Advance Praise for MAKING CHANGE

"Even great dreamers need imagination to achieve their goals. When you visualize, you open yourself up to the help of the universe. *Making Change* is a new 'hands-on' book full of very useful ways to achieve personal and organizational goals. The fact that Bilaal has been able to produce such a piece of work with such clarity and discipline of mind is just outstanding."

—LIEUTENANT-GENERAL THE HONOURABLE ROMÉO DALLAIRE, (RET'D), SENATOR

"We often refer to young people as 'the leaders of tomorrow.' But more and more, the youth of the world are showing us they can truly be the leaders of today. *Making Change* reminds us that there's no need to wait."

—CRAIG KIELBURGER, FOUNDER AND CHAIR OF FREE THE CHILDREN

"I've known Bilaal for many years. *Making Change* is both a road map, showing the route he has traveled, and an invitation for others to follow. He is an inspiration, a role model, a dynamo and one of my heroes."

—ERIC WALTERS, AUTHOR AND ACTIVIST

MAKING CHANGE

Tips from an Underage Overachiever

BILAAL RAJAN

ORCA BOOK PUBLISHERS

Library and Archives Canada Cataloguing in Publication

Rajan, Bilaal, 1996-
Making change : tips from an underage overachiever / written by Bilaal Rajan.

ISBN 978-1-55469-001-5

1. Fund raising--Juvenile literature. I. Title.

HV41.2.R36 2008   j361.7068'1   C2008-903061-3

First published in the United States, 2008

Library of Congress Control Number: 2008928579

Summary: Motivation, inspiration and fundraising tips from UNICEF Canada Child Representative.

Orca Book Publishers gratefully acknowledges the support for its publishing programs provided by the following agencies: the Government of Canada through the Book Publishing Industry Development Program and the Canada Council for the Arts, and the Province of British Columbia through the BC Arts Council and the Book Publishing Tax Credit.

Cover and text design by Teresa Bubela
Workbook pages by Bruce Collins
Cover photo of Bilaal Rajan (top) © Michael Peake, *Toronto Sun* photographer, reprinted with the permission of Sun Media Corporation
Cover photo of Bilaal Rajan (bottom) © UNICEF Canada
Author photo by Moez Vizram

All interior photographs courtesy of the Rajan family or UNICEF Canada unless otherwise noted.

ORCA BOOK PUBLISHERS
PO Box 5626, STN. B
VICTORIA, BC CANADA
V8R 6S4

ORCA BOOK PUBLISHERS
PO Box 468
CUSTER, WA USA
98240-0468

www.orcabook.com
Printed and bound in Canada.

11 10 09 08 • 4 3 2 1

To His Highness Prince Karim Al-Husseini Aga Khan, a man who, for the last fifty years, has worked tirelessly for the uplift and betterment of all the world's citizens. Happy Golden Jubilee!

"There are many interpretations of Islam within the wider Islamic community, but generally we are instructed to leave the world a better place than it was when we came into it."
—HIS HIGHNESS PRINCE KARIM AL-HUSSEINI AGA KHAN

"There are those who enter the world in such poverty that they are deprived of both the means and the motivation to improve their lot. Unless they can be touched with the spark which ignites the spirit of individual enterprise and determination, they will only sink into apathy, degradation and despair. It is for us, who are more fortunate, to provide that spark."
—HIS HIGHNESS PRINCE KARIM AL-HUSSEINI AGA KHAN

How it all began. Age four, with father, Aman Rajan

Acknowledgments

First and foremost, I would like to thank my mom and dad, Shamim and Aman Rajan, for all their love and support. From day one they have been there for me, along with my grandparents, Zarina and Mansur Rajan.

My friend Eric Walters encouraged my writing and put me in contact with Bob Tyrrell and Andrew Wooldridge at Orca Book Publishers. I am grateful to them for believing in me. Thank you, too, to my editor, Sarah Harvey, who helped me smooth the book out and kept me on a tight time leash; otherwise this never would have been completed. I am grateful to Art Director Teresa Bubela for creating such an attractive and readable design. Lastly, thanks to the marketing manager, Dayle Sutherland, and the marketing team for spreading the word.

At my school, St. Andrew's College in Aurora, Ontario, many people contribute to my education and support my endeavors. I would particularly like to thank Headmaster Ted Staunton and Middle School Director Mike Hanson for believing in me and supporting me in all my creative endeavors. Thanks also to Michael Roy and Dolly Moffat Lynch, Kim Sillcox, Sarah Dame and my grade six Language Arts teacher, Alyson Bartlett, who inspired me and gave me confidence. She liked my story so much that she wanted it to be published—and here it is!

At UNICEF Canada, there are a lot of people who help me: Nigel and Jennifer Fisher, Alan Ely, Mr. and Mrs. Dwight Mihalicz, Amy Tong, John Humble, Jackie Jones, Kari Sackney and Nicole Ireland. Thank you all.

Rick Comtois, Dawn Larsen, Adil Lalani, Galib Rayani and Tammi Winchester help me keep my life in balance and give me unconditional support.

I am very grateful to everyone who has supported me: donors, supporters, well-wishers and mentors who have helped me all along the way, from the early days of clementine sales, to being UNICEF Canada Child Representative, to helping make this book a reality. Together we HAVE made a difference.

Contents

Left to right: Amy Tong, Bilaal, Nigel Fisher

Foreword

Nigel Fisher
PRESIDENT AND CEO, UNICEF CANADA

How often have you heard that you are the future? Of course that's true, but you are also the present. Your life is not waiting to begin at some future date—when you graduate, can legally drive a car or vote. Your life is well underway—right now.

Often when adults think of children, they think in terms of untapped potential, of young people who will be the citizens of a tomorrow that is still years away. When opinion leaders and political leaders consider climate change and global warming, they ask, "What kind of world will we leave for our children and grandchildren?" But if you are like many young people I know, you are looking at the world around you and saying, "I can see right now the dangers to our environment. And if I can already see what is happening, the real question is: What are we doing today—this hour, this minute—to ensure a sustainable world?" The future does not depend only on future action; it is a direct result of the decisions and actions we take today.

A sustainable world is also one in which there is justice—not just for the lucky few, but for people everywhere. It is a world in which poverty is not acceptable, where we offer a helpful hand to people struggling to better their future. It is a world in which children everywhere have that most basic of rights: the right not to die from a preventable disease.

It is a world where they are protected from exploitation, and where they can go to school and get a good-quality education. Yet millions of children around the world die needlessly every year from diseases like pneumonia or malaria; millions of children are exploited as child laborers or trafficked across borders; millions—including children right here in Canada—are deprived of a decent education.

These things don't have to happen. And you can help do something about them. That is Bilaal Rajan's message in this book—act now!

You might scratch your head and ask, "But what can I do?" Well, Bilaal has a few suggestions—actually, he has a lot of suggestions and a lot of experience. He started raising money for earthquake victims at the age of four, and he has since been the key to raising millions for many causes. He travels the world so that he can help other children directly. And now, not yet in his teens, he has some words of advice and lots of great ideas about how you too can make a difference, right now, to the world around you. Now, that's something worth reading about! By the time you have finished chapter two of Bilaal's book, you will already have at least ninety-four fundraising ideas!

Much of my work around the world for UNICEF has been in countries at war or recovering from war—Afghanistan, Iraq, Rwanda, Mozambique, to name a few. Children always suffer the most in times of war: they are uprooted from their homes, separated from their families, orphaned, or traumatized by the terrible scenes of mayhem that they witness. People often ask me, "When you see so much suffering, don't you ever lose hope? How can you remain an optimist?" My response is simple—you can always make a difference. Optimism is the only option. You have to believe that there is hope, and that you can help create that hope. You can take joy in working with your team to help ensure that people have shelter, food and clean water, that children are vaccinated against killer diseases, that they can recover from the traumatic events which they have suffered, and that they can be reunited with their loved ones. Above all, you don't just wring your hands in despair. You take action—you must believe that you can make a difference and, indeed, you can see that difference in action all around you.

Bilaal's message is simple: you can make a difference right now. In fact, his motto is: "Together We Can Make a Difference." You don't have to go to a far-off country to do so. Right here, today, in your school, in your community, you can help those who may not be as fortunate as you are; you can make the world a better place. Read this book and the ideas for action will start rattling around your brain.

Bilaal has lots of ideas and his life is inspiring. See the sections entitled "Bilaal's Way" scattered throughout the book for concrete examples of what he has done to help others. But I bet that his book will also trigger some of your very own ideas too—for fundraising and for getting involved in making our world a better place.

As you read *Making Change*, you will pick up some really good tips: how to think big; why goals are important and how to set them; why working with others beats trying to do everything on your own; how to become aware of and understand other people's passions, thoughts and emotions. When you see something from someone else's perspective, that's called empathy. Bilaal will also help you become an "active listener" as you become an activist. And you'll find out about things like "sticky goals" when you work your way through Bilaal's Eight Principles To Maximize Your True Potential!

As a UNICEF Canada Child Representative, Bilaal has inspired thousands of Canadians, young and old, to get involved in helping children in the developing world to have a better life. He has been the inspiration behind campaigns that have raised millions of dollars for UNICEF's programs for children worldwide. But don't be intimidated. His message is straightforward and practical: Figure out what gets you excited, find your passion, and then do something about it. Think big, begin small. Visualize success. You can achieve your goals. Success builds confidence—and further success.

Read on and be inspired. You are the future of the world—and the future begins now. So act now. Not next week or next month; not tomorrow, but today.

Nigel Fisher

TORONTO

MAY 2008

With children in Malawi

Introduction

Enthusiasm is excitement with inspiration,
motivation, and a pinch of creativity.

—BO BENNETT, PHILANTHROPIST, MOTIVATIONAL SPEAKER
AND AUTHOR

You probably think you cannot build a home or a school from clementine oranges, but let me tell you how it can be done. Near the end of January 2001, there was a terrible earthquake in Gujarat, an Indian state. In that part of the world most people live in big towns and cities, which were shaken violently. Cracks appeared in the earth, people's houses were destroyed, and schools and hospitals crumbled. Many thousands of people were killed as buildings collapsed on top of them.

I was only four years old when this happened, but the news of the destruction had a big impact on me. My parents told me about the earthquake as they were reading the newspaper. A *jamatkhana* (an Ismaili Muslim center of prayer or worship that is kept peaceful and holy) had collapsed under the force of the earthquake and the *mukhisaheb*, or priest, had died. He had young children of his own, who were just a little older than I was. My parents were leaders in our *jamatkhana* in Richmond Hill, Ontario, at the time. I thought about what would become of me if a disaster like that happened here. I could be left without parents.

When I thought about what had happened in Gujarat, I imagined the devastation. I was eating a clementine orange while I was thinking about the earthquake, and I was trying to think how I could help. Then, as I bit into the juicy fruit, it came to me. Sell clementines! Now all I had to do was get to work.

I felt very confident when I first went out with my box of clementines. I was going to sell from door to door in a community not too far from of my house. I always had an adult with me—one of my parents or a grandparent. Some people said no to me, but I did not stop. After all, many people said yes. My parents taught me that you should always keep trying. Giving up is never the solution. When I was finished selling clementines, I had raised $350, which is a lot of money to a four-year-old.

I'm not exactly sure what motivated me to do what I did. Yes, I imagined what it would be like if this tragedy had happened to my family, but it was still very far removed from me. What was more important is that I was INSPIRED to help the children who had been left alone, without parents. I was inspired by their suffering, and I sought a solution that I thought might help ease that suffering.

What is the difference between motivation and inspiration? Easy. Motivation is something that comes from inside you, and inspiration comes from the outside. Of course, there is nothing wrong with motivation. It drives us to accomplish great things. However, without inspiration our actions can often be empty. The person who has inspired me the most is our spiritual leader, His Highness the Aga Khan. He is a philanthropist who has devoted himself to bettering the lives of others around the world. For more information about the Aga Khan, please visit www.akdn.org.

During the years that followed, I did a lot more fundraising and public speaking, and I could see that there were many kids who cared and who wanted to fundraise with me and make a difference in the world. I also knew that, although I was constantly being labeled as "special," there was nothing I had that lots of other kids didn't have. Each and every one of them had the potential to do anything they chose to do.

You all have this type of potential inside of you, just waiting to get out. What you need are the tools to bring out that potential and make it shine. No matter whether you want to excel in school, fundraise, work to earn extra money or help your family through hard times, you can do it if you know how to tap into the potential that is inside you.

So why did I write this book? Because I want to inspire others the way His Highness the Aga Khan and many others have inspired me. I know that there are many kids who want to know how to raise funds. I want kids to find their passion, take action and know that they can do amazing things and make a difference in the lives of others. It's not difficult. If you believe in your cause, and you know that what you are doing is right, you will be able to raise funds, and you should do it. Never lose confidence. Everyone has to find their passion. It may be fundraising to help kids on the other side of the world, it may be helping animals, helping the elderly in nursing homes, helping the physically challenged—there are hundreds of worthy causes. I have concentrated on helping kids. I feel kids need to help other kids. Children are the creators and leaders of our future. I believe that there should be equality and fairness for all children. Why shouldn't children in other parts of the world have exactly what we have here in North America? Things like clean water, education, clothing, food, toys, all the things we take for granted. I chose to work with UNICEF, which stands for United Nations Children's Fund, because they work specifically with children to provide basic education, clean water and food.

This book is divided into two parts: the first section concentrates on fundraising; the second part is meant to help you reach your full potential.

The following pages are full of my experiences, which I hope not only inspire you, but also give you direction and help you decide what concrete actions to take. You can take these methods and apply them to any fundraising or humanitarian efforts in which you are involved. Just remember—YOU CAN DO IT!

Fundraising with Ilahi Rayani (PHOTO GALIB RAYANI)

PART I

Fundraising Tips for Activist Kids

Selling clementines at age four with mother, Shamim Rajan

CHAPTER 1

You CAN Do Amazing Things

Whatever you can do, or dream you can, begin it.
Boldness has genius, power, and magic in it.
—JOHANN WOLFGANG VON GOETHE, GERMAN AUTHOR AND PHILOSOPHER

Getting Started

FIND YOUR PASSION

You really **can** do amazing things. So many people are afraid to think big. Many are afraid to think about doing anything at all. They feel that since they can't do **everything**, they will do **nothing**. And then there are those who don't even know where to begin. You can be different. Think about what you believe in. What are your values? How do you want to make a difference in the world? Of course, after you have answered these questions, getting started is the biggest step you will ever take.

When I began fundraising at the age of four, I did not think in terms of how I wanted to make a difference in the world. I simply knew that there were children suffering because of a horrible natural disaster, and I knew that I wanted to help them. I also did not think it was amazing or unusual that I was fundraising. It was simply an effort to make the lives of other children better. I just did what I knew I had to do.

I think this is the key. Go out there with a specific need in mind. No one person ALONE can change the whole world. Just let a cause or a certain situation or group of people inspire you, and give it all you've got.

That's what I did, and I made a difference. Think of it this way. How do you start a fire? All it takes is one spark, right? Just one little spark and you can start a huge fire. As Mahatma Gandhi once said, "Be the change you want to see in the world."

DO YOUR RESEARCH

Of course, you can't just go out on the street or start calling people up and say you are raising money for HIV/AIDS victims in Malawi. You need to know about the cause you are raising funds for. As I said, start with a cause that inspires you. If you don't care about it, you won't be able to convince others of its importance. Once you know what you want to support, you have to learn all you can about it. When you ask people for money to support a cause, they won't just hand it over. They will want to know about the cause: why it is important, who is affected by it, and how their money will help make a difference.

Get on the Internet and read about your cause. Be prepared to answer the five "W" questions:

- **Who**—Who is already involved in your cause? Who needs to be involved to help you reach your goal? Who benefits from you reaching your goal? Whose lives do you wish to affect?
- **What**—What is it that you want to accomplish? What requirements are necessary to accomplish your goal? What might get in the way of achieving your goal?
- **Where**—What location is associated with your cause?
- **When**—What is the time frame for your goal? This is especially important. You need to set a completion date and stick to it as best you can.
- **Why**—Why are you doing this? What is your motivation and/or inspiration? In other words, what are the reasons for, or purposes behind, your goal?

MAKE A POSTER

After you have answered the five "W" questions, make a poster to remind you every day of what you want to do and why. This will help you stay motivated.

When you can speak to someone intelligently about your cause, you will be more likely to gain their support, and you may be surprised how supportive some people can be. Of course, you will always have the support of your family and friends. After all, Grandma can't resist you, right? But you can only raise so much money from just family and friends. You have to go beyond them, and that is when you need to know your stuff.

Do It for the Right Reasons

If you are thinking of fundraising as a way of gaining recognition and having people like you, then I recommend you think again. Fundraising is a serious endeavor, and I strongly feel that whatever you undertake, you must not do it lightly. The real reason to raise funds or be an activist is to HELP OTHERS. If you have any other goals in mind, please take the time to rethink them. When your heart is in the right place, the sky's the limit. It is also true that if you do good things selflessly, good things will happen to you. Find your calling. Your calling may not be fundraising. It may be giving your time as a volunteer. For example, a couple of years ago, I decided I wanted to interact face-to-face with children in developing countries. I wanted to lend a hand, rather than just work as a fundraiser. I wanted to support and empower the kids, and give them hope.

In February 2005, I had the honor of being appointed UNICEF Canada Child Representative. I gladly accepted, because I knew it was a great way to help children. It was also a good way to spread my message of hope. Some people may think that being a UNICEF child ambassador is just about being a poster boy—looking good and appearing on the front pages of newspapers—but I was, and still am, actively involved in raising money and awareness. The point is that everything I do—from selling clementines to working for UNICEF—is about helping kids and inspiring others to help as well. When children see that I can do it, they know that they can do it too—and they do.

I have spoken with a lot of young people who want to help. Some of the kids are younger than I am and some are older. I have spoken to kids across Canada and in the United States, as well as in many other countries such as Malawi, Tanzania, Sri Lanka, Thailand and the Maldives.

All this recognition shows me that I am making a difference and that what I have to say is being heard. I am no more gifted or capable than you are. I just acted on my desire to help. You have a voice that can be just as loud. You don't have to be really outgoing or even very talkative to do this kind of work. Silent messages are often the loudest ones of all. You can talk to people all you want about helping out or about your value system or what is important to you, but the message doesn't always get through. However, when you are taking action and living your message, it gets through loud and clear, and it inspires people more than words ever could.

Think about it. Do you think Gandhi would have had such an impact on the world with his words alone? Of course, his words are wise beyond measure, but if he just sat in a room and spoke those words without ever DOING anything, would people really have noticed him?

You are Raising More than Money

When you go out and raise money for a cause, you are helping people by giving them material goods or the money to buy these goods. However, you are doing so much more than that. When you go out there and ask for support, you are raising AWARENESS for a cause. When you raise awareness, so much can be done. It can often inspire other people to come up with their own unique ways to help out. You also let the people you are raising money for realize that they are not alone and that other people in the world care about them.

This means that you are also raising spirits. The people you are trying to help are flesh and blood; they have feelings, just like you. You are affecting their lives deeply when you work hard to raise funds for them.

If you ever doubt yourself and your capabilities, then please say to yourself "I can do anything! I can make a difference!" Just take the time right now to think of one thing that is important to you, one area in which you would like to help others and make a difference. Do you know where to begin? Do you know what you can do to help? Talk it over with a trusted and supportive adult, and then DO something AMAZING!

Fundraising for Haiti with Ella Wardlaw

With students from Creighton Park Elementary, Dartmouth, Nova Scotia

CHAPTER 2

Get Creative

Every great inspiration is but an experiment.
—CHARLES IVES, AMERICAN COMPOSER

Part of the reason for writing this book is to encourage others to raise funds for those in need. If you think fundraising is only about going door-to-door to ask for money or asking people and organizations for donations, think again. Not only have I sold clementines and cookies to raise money, I have also taken part in charity walks such as the World Partnership Walk. The World Partnership Walk is an effort to eliminate global poverty; one hundred percent of funds raised go to the cause. I have been able raise over $1,000 each year since I was four. In 2005 I raised over $12,000 single-handedly, and my team total came to over $17,000. It is pretty amazing to see a whole event run just by volunteers. There are many other charitable walks and runs that you can get involved in. You can do lots of other things to raise money. For instance, I took a photography class at a summer camp. Later, I took pictures when I was on vacation in Hawaii. I then sold these pictures on eBay to raise funds for UNICEF.

If you give it some thought, you can come up with your own schemes for helping those in need. Many fundraisers—like bake sales and bottle drives—are easy to organize, but add something different, and you'll get great results. A book sale is a simple and direct way to raise funds, but you can make it a bit special too. For example, I invited Eric Walters, a popular writer of books for children and young adults, to come to my school to help raise money for UNICEF. People paid to listen to him talk, and the money went to children in need. I already knew Eric Walters because he had come to my home once to interview me for one of his books. We kept in touch, so he was happy to do the talk. Think about someone you or your family knows who might add something special to your fundraising efforts.

Different ideas appeal to different types of people. This means it's not a good idea just to do the same thing over and over again, year after year, although many large organizations do that successfully. Try to change the format depending on what you think will appeal to the people you are asking for donations.

There are as many ways to raise funds for a cause as there are people. You would be amazed at the number and variety of ways in which you can raise funds for your cause. I have created a list of fundraising ideas. Take a look. Feel free to use ideas from my list and create your own variations.

These ideas are designed to trigger your imagination. Please do not forget to think about safety concerns as you make your plans. You may also need a bit of help financially before you start, to buy supplies, print posters etc. Seek permission where necessary, and involve adults (parents/guardians, friends and teachers) in your plans. The most important thing is to have fun while you help others!

Fundraising Ideas

ATHLETIC

1. **Walk-a-thon:** This is a great way to get people out in support of a cause. People can laugh and socialize while raising money for your cause. Simply choose a date and a route, make up some pledge forms and advertise with posters. Have everyone who wants to participate gather donations or pledges using the pledge forms.

2. **Skip-a-thon:** Everyone loves skipping. Follow the same guidelines as a walkathon, and then skip, skip, skip!

3. **Pitch-a-thon/kick-a-thon:** Rent a radar gun and measure how fast people can throw a baseball or kick a soccer ball. Charge $1 per try and give a prize to the fastest individual.

4. **Three-on-three basketball tournament:** Organize a basketball tournament in your school with the winning team receiving a donated prize. This can also be done with soccer, tennis, badminton or any other sport. Charge an entry fee and sell tickets to the event.

5. **Beat the goalie:** Pick the best hockey or soccer goalie you know and invite people to try to score a goal for a prize. Participants must pay to play.

6. **Bowling:** Organize a bowling night or a competition. Ask a bowling alley to donate the use of a couple of lanes. Charge everyone a small fee to enter, or have participants get bowl-a-thon pledges.

7. **Sporting events tickets:** Ask sports teams to donate seats for their games, and then raffle off the tickets.

8. **Miniature golf:** Ask your school principal if you can build a nine-hole miniature golf course at your school, featuring ramps, water, sand traps, and other obstacles. Charge people to play a round during lunch.

9. **Bench-a-thon:** Have people bench-press weights in the school gym, and collect pledges for every kilogram they lift. This is a popular event, especially with football players. Make sure all participants have spotters to ensure safety.

10. **Sports tournament/fitness competition:** Organize a sports tournament or fitness competition. Advertise well and charge spectators to come and watch groups compete. You may need to have medical personnel on hand.

11. **Triathlon:** Set a course of running, cycling and swimming. Have participants get pledges to compete to win prizes.

AT YOUR SCHOOL

12. **Raffles:** People love raffles. You can raffle off just about anything. Sell tickets and keep the ticket stubs. On the date of the draw, have someone not involved in the fundraising pick a ticket stub from all the ones that were sold. Do this publicly.

13. **Jellybean count:** Fill a jar with jellybeans and have people pay to guess how many there are in the jar. The money goes to your cause and the winner gets the jelly beans.

14. **Dress-down/civvies day:** If you attend a school that requires a uniform, get permission to have a day on which students can wear casual clothes. Charge each student who wants to participate.

15. **Band and choir concerts:** Ask your school band or choir to donate their time by performing a benefit concert for your cause. Charge admission for the event and let the entertainment begin.

16. **Spelling bee:** Come up with a list of words of increasing difficulty. Have people pay to participate and to watch. Or have a geography-themed bee using place names.

17. **Battle of the bands:** Talk to some bands in your community. Book the school gym and advertise with posters, flyers and radio announcements. Charge admission to a mini-concert in which the audience chooses the winning band.

18. **Piñata contest:** Charge a fee to let blindfolded people have one turn at trying to break a candy-filled piñata. Whoever breaks the piñata gets to keep the candy.

19. **Monopoly match:** Charge students to participate in a Monopoly tournament, with the winner receiving a donated prize.

20. **Guess the age of your teachers:** Organize an event in which students pay to guess the age of their teachers. However, please obtain approval from the teachers first!

21. **Hoopla:** Competitors throw Hula hoops over prizes. The person whose hoop completely lands over the prize gets to keep the prize. Make sure you do not spend too much money on prizes.

22. **Debate evening:** Research a number of debate issues and invite various community members to debate the issues. Charge the audience to come and watch. The issues can be fun. For example, have your school principal argue that listening to music during class enhances a student's ability to learn; have a student argue that music should be banned from school.

23. **Comedy hour:** Host a comedy skit during lunch at your school and charge people to attend. You can ask friends to help you perform the skit or you can do it yourself.

24. **Popcorn party:** Sell bags of popcorn during lunch.

25. **Ugly tie contest:** Charge a small fee for students to come to school wearing the ugliest tie they can find. Other students can pay to vote for the ugliest tie. The winner receives a prize.

26. **Crazy hat day:** Students pay a fee to wear a crazy hat to school for the day; other students pay to vote for the craziest hat.

27. **"Get-out-of-jail-free" card:** Students pay to get out of a class period for a day. Ask permission from teachers or principals first; of course, the students have to make up the work missed.

28. **Game show:** Recreate one or more of your favorite game shows, and charge contestants and audience a small entrance fee.

29. **Sit in a bath:** Obtain sponsorship for kids to sit in a tub of something gross or out of the ordinary, such as baked beans or fruit-flavored gelatin.

30. **Talent show competition:** Charge students a small fee to show off their talents in a lunch-hour competition. Sell tickets and give everyone an opportunity to vote for their favorite performer.

31. **Hand art:** Decorate people's hands with henna (Indian hand art) or do nail-painting for a fee.

IN YOUR COMMUNITY

32. **Auction:** Ask individuals, groups and businesses to donate goods and services. Be creative in what you auction off, and make certain that you start the bidding at reasonable prices.

33. **Bag groceries:** Ask a local grocery store if you can bag people's groceries for donations. Be sure to put up a sign saying what the donation is for.

34. **Perform a service for a donation:** Rake leaves, shovel snow, take care of a pet. When offering your service, ask for a donation toward your worthy cause.

35. **Sell candy or cards:** Ask reputable businesses to provide merchandise at wholesale prices. Donate the profits to your cause.

36. **Sell buttons or T-shirts displaying your logo:** Create a logo for your cause and print it on T-shirts, buttons or pens. (You may need a bit of help with start-up costs. Ask merchants to donate items too.) Sell the items at a reasonable price and put the profits toward your cause.

37. **Puppet show:** Make puppets with socks, felt and other craft materials. Pick out or write your own story. Set a date, time and location, and advertise with flyers and posters. Sell tickets and let the show begin.

38. **Spaghetti dinner:** Prepare a great dinner (it doesn't have to be spaghetti) for students, teachers or community members, and charge a fee.

39. **Hold a theme party:** Decide on a fun theme—togas or superheroes or the seventies. Charge an entrance fee, but be sure to explain to people what their cover charge is going toward.

40. **Newsletter:** Create a newsletter informing your peers and members of your community about your organization or cause. Sell the newsletter for a small fee. Be sure to provide information about how people can become involved and/or donate to your cause. And make sure to include some fun stuff too.

41. **Plant a tree:** Ask a nursery for seedling donations and then get people to sponsor a tree. Ask your local parks department where you can plant the trees. Have a planting party for all those who donated, and ask the media to announce and cover your event.

42. **Endurance contests:** Gather pledges for a dance-a-thon, rock-a-thon, swim-a-thon or any other type of endurance contest you can think of.

43. **Day of community service:** Gather together a group of friends and contact organizations who need volunteers. Then have people sponsor you to do community service for a set number of hours.

44. **Food fast:** Get together with a group of friends, gather pledges, and fast for a full twenty-four hours. Make sure parents and/or doctors give their permission.

45. **Craft sale:** Make all the crafts yourself and sell them. You can also ask other kids or adults to donate things they have made.

46. **Family barbecue:** Host a family barbecue or potluck in your backyard, with games and activities. Ask family members for donations to your cause.

47. **Bingo:** Host a bingo night at a local hall, place of worship or school.

48. **Plant sale:** Organize a plant sale with plants donated by local nurseries.

49. **Games night:** Organize an evening of board games and have the people who want to participate pay or give a donation.

50. **Boat race:** Organize a model boat race. Charge a participant/spectator entrance fee. The winner of the race gets a donated prize.

51. **Fruit stand:** Get permission to go to local farms and pick fruit to sell. Sell the produce in high-traffic areas or at community festivals.

52. **Book sale:** Ask all your friends, relatives, and teachers to donate their old books. Advertise by means of posters and flyers. Set up a table in your school in a classroom, hallway or lunchroom, and sell books. If there are leftovers, you can always give them to a library, shelter or school.

53. **Buy a brick:** If you are fundraising to build a school or building, have people make donations to purchase bricks or other building materials.

54. **Petting zoo:** If you live in an area where there are farms nearby, organize a one-day petting zoo for children, or try to find an animal rescue farm in your area and visit the animals there.

55. **Coupon sale:** Sell coupon books donated by local businesses.

56. **International dinner:** Ask people from various ethnicities and cultures to cook their traditional foods and then charge admission to an international dinner.

57. **Balloon pop:** Before filling balloons with air or helium, put notes inside. A certain number of the notes will be worth a prize. Ask people to buy balloons and pop them in the hope of getting the prize. Be sure to pick up the broken balloons afterward.

58. **Scavenger hunt:** Set a route and make a list of items that the participants need to find in order to win. Advertise your scavenger hunt well, and charge everyone a small fee to participate. The winning person/group gets a prize.

59. **Car wash:** With a group of friends, set up a car wash in the parking lot of your school, church or a local garage. Be sure to ask for permission, and stay safe around moving cars.

60. **Candle making:** Make candles and sell them to family members or at craft fairs. This can be educational and fun, but be sure to exercise all safety precautions and work with an adult.

61. **Charity ball:** Hire a DJ or a band, rent a hall, advertise, and sell tickets for a dance.

62. **Classic car show:** Organize a classic automobile show at a community center or school parking lot. Place ads in local newspapers, leave flyers at local businesses and charge people to come and see the show.

63. **Clearing snow:** Shovel snow from people's driveways and walkways in the winter months for a donation.

64. **Dog show:** Invite people to pay a small fee to show off their dogs at a local community center. Charge a small admission fee and offer a prize for the best-groomed dog, most- and least-obedient dog, and so on.

65. **Talent auction:** Auction off people's talents. For instance, offer to have great singers sing at a wedding or party, or get a chef to cook a special dinner for the winning bidder.

66. **Duck race:** Sell numbered plastic ducks. Set all the ducks afloat in a race on a river or lake. The person who bought the duck that wins the race gets a prize.

67. **Guess the number of pennies in a jar:** The winner receives all the coins and your group makes money by charging people for guessing.

68. **Eating marathon:** Have a pie-eating, hot-dog-eating, or ice-cream-eating contest. You can charge people to participate or to watch, or you can ask participants to obtain pledges. Make sure to get parental permission and have medical personnel on hand.

69. **Face painting:** Advertise in advance and then charge a small fee for painting little kids' faces at a community or sporting event.

70. **Flower show:** Invite gardeners from your community to enter their flowers in a competition for a prize. Ask volunteer experts to be judges, and charge all participants and spectators a fee.

71. **Calendar sale:** Create a calendar highlighting the projects and members of your organization and sell it to students, family members and the community.

72. **Art sale:** Ask local artists to donate their works to be displayed and sold in your school or at your local community center.

73. **Gardening:** Mow lawns, weed or water gardens for neighbors and friends for a donation.

74. **Guest speaker:** Invite a guest speaker to your home, school or local hall. Sell admission tickets to raise funds for your cause.

75. **Karaoke:** Rent a karaoke machine, charge an admission fee and sing all night.

76. **Videos:** When you travel, make videos for other youth travelers. Or create a how-to video—for example, how to improve your golf swing or how to make crafts.

77. **Miles of coins:** Gather donations of coins and lay them side-by-side until they surround your library, school, home or parking lot. Take photos of your coins and send the pictures to local media. The longer your coin trail, the better your donation for your cause. See if you can get in *Guinness World Records*.

78. **Recipe book:** Gather favorite recipes and put them together in a book. Sell the book through your school, sports organization

or community center. Try to get the photocopying donated by local businesses.

79. **Pet care:** Walk dogs, feed cats or clean out birdcages for a small fee.

80. **Toy sale:** Ask for donations of gently used toys and sell them for a small donation.

SEASONAL

81. **New Year's snow art contest.** Charge people to participate and to vote for their favorite snow art.

82. **Hold a Valentine's Day dance.**

83. **Hold a St. Patrick's Day car wash.**

84. **Sell flowers for Valentine's Day and Mother's Day.** Ask local flower shops and nurseries to donate flowers.

85. **Get donations of hot dogs and hamburgers** from local shops and hold a **Father's Day barbecue.**

86. **Celebrate Canada Day** with festivities, entertainment and refreshment/food booths.

87. **Make lemonade** on a hot day, post signs and sell it to passersby.

88. **Say good-bye to summer with an end-of-summer party** at your local pool. Charge an entrance fee and make sure you have adult supervision at all times.

89. **Hold a back-to-school dance** or get donations of supplies and **hold a back-to-school supplies sale.**

90. **Hold a Thanksgiving turkey raffle.**

91. **Pumpkin-decorating contest:** Around Halloween, hold a pumpkin-decorating contest at your school. Break the contest up into categories according to age. Display the pumpkins and charge a small fee for students and staff to vote for their favorite pumpkin.

92. **Winter carnival:** Hold a winter carnival in your local park or schoolyard. Invite students, staff and the community. Charge admission and/or a small fee to play games. You could also host a mini-carnival any time of the year, with games, prizes and popcorn

in a local park or your own backyard. Make sure to ask permission first.

93. **Carol singing:** During the Christmas season, go door-to-door singing carols for donations. It is a good idea to hand out a card or a flyer with some brief information about your organization. You may want to have an adult accompany you. Remember to respect those who do not celebrate Christmas and who may not want to hear your carols.

94. **Christmas ornament sale:** Sell Christmas ornaments during the Christmas season. You can either make them yourself or ask others to make them.

This is just the beginning. By knowing your own community, you can come up with your own ideas or try variations on mine. Whatever group you have decided to help will benefit from your efforts and so will you. As a fundraiser, you can be a true leader in your school, your classroom, your church or any other community in which you are involved. Whatever you do, you will know for sure that you are helping people who really need your help—people who don't have clean water or food or the luxuries that we take for granted here. You can help make their lives a lot better just by deciding on a goal and then putting it into action.

BILAAL'S WAY Plates A-Plenty!

I love doing science experiments. In December 2004 my mom bought me a science project that was basically a kit that allowed you to make acrylic plates out of beads. It was an interesting process, and the finished plates were pretty neat—very colorful and decorative as well as being quite practical too.

At first I gave the plates to my aunt, who kept them in her home. Then, with the holidays coming, I decided to give some to my teachers as Christmas presents. They were a bit different from the usual presents teachers get.

Then I thought, why don't I sell them to raise money for children living with HIV/AIDS? I tried selling them at the big train station, Union Station, first, since I had had success selling cookies in that location. It was very cold and there was a lot of snow. I didn't sell many plates, and one plate even cracked because it was so cold.

However, I don't give up easily. I tried to find a place to sell my plates but there was already too much going on because of the Christmas rush, and some places wanted me to have a permit and insurance.

Things were not going so well, but finally I contacted a coffee shop in downtown Toronto and—success! They let me in. In fact, they did more than that—they very kindly gave me space and a table so I could set up a booth. My parents were there too, keeping an eye on me. I spoke to customers as they walked in and got very good results. People seemed to like the idea of a kid raising money for other kids. Also, I had a lot of help from the people at CityTV/Pulse 24 News. They made the public aware of my efforts by announcing where I was and what I was doing. Their support was very helpful and important to me. In three days of selling my handmade plates for three hours each day, I raised about $1,200 for children living with HIV/AIDS.

Because of the good reviews and publicity, one man came looking for me so he could buy a plate for his girlfriend for her birthday. She had seen me on TV and really wanted one. The normal price for a plate was $25. This man paid eight times the price—$200 for a plate, because he wanted to help combat HIV/AIDS. And that wasn't all. Another man came by and bought ten plates, which was really amazing.

I found it really encouraging that people believed that fundraising for children with HIV/AIDS is important. If you are inspired to raise funds for any worthwhile cause, don't let anything stop you. No matter what. Are you feeling too sick or too busy to fundraise? Then get a team together. You already know a lot of people who could be members. Let them help you. Do whatever you can to help out if you believe in the cause.

I don't always know exactly what to do the first time I try something. You might be nervous in the beginning, but you will become confident as you get more experience. You can learn from your experiences—when things go wrong, as well as when they go right. Think about what happened, and make changes to your methods if you think there is room for improvement. If I could do those plates a second time, I would sell them on eBay and on my website, but I still think a personal encounter is best if you can manage it.

Selling handmade acrylic plates for UNICEF

Thanking Jack Kay, president and COO *of Apotex,*
for a large donation of medicine

CHAPTER 3

Think Big

Aim for the moon. If you miss, you may hit a star.
—W. CLEMENT STONE, SELF-HELP BOOK GURU AND
FATHER OF POSITIVE MENTAL ATTITUDE™

D on't ever let anyone tell you that you can't reach your fundraising goals. If you want to aim high, then go for it! The sky's the limit. Whatever you set out to do is achievable as long as you believe it can be done and you have a support network in place to help you along the way. Oh, and of course you have to do the work. I think it is easy for people to follow the norm and shoot for a "reasonable" goal. But who's to say what is reasonable? If you have the ability and the ambition to go beyond that, then do it!

Another very important reason to think big is that even if you fall short of your goal, you will still be farther ahead than if you hadn't tried at all. If you aim to raise $100, you will do it, for sure. However, if you aim to raise $1,000, you can probably do that too. But say you only raise $500? Well, that's $400 more than $100, isn't it?

The following is a plan for setting goals. It is called the SMART plan. I use it as much as I can, and it works! Many years ago, a man named Peter Drucker came up with this way of evaluating objectives and setting goals in his book, *The Practice of Management*. A SMART objective is one that is specific, measurable, achievable, realistic and timely. It really helps make goal-setting easy.

$$S — \text{Specific}$$
$$M — \text{Measurable}$$
$$A — \text{Achievable}$$
$$R — \text{Realistic}$$
$$T — \text{Timely}$$

SPECIFIC

If your goal is too general, then it will be much more difficult to accomplish. You must have a detailed vision. Remember the five "W" questions? (page 2) This is a good opportunity to use them to figure out exactly what you need to do. For instance, if what you really want is to get a reading prize from school, don't just say you want to get good grades in English. Make sure you know how many books you need to read and how much time you have to complete the task. Then get reading!

MEASURABLE

This means that you must be able to see progress and chart it. Of course, when you have met your goal, you will know it, but it is very useful and motivational to set small measurable milestones along the way. Ideally you want to see change occurring at each stage of your journey. Instead of saying, "I want to raise money to help UNICEF," which is not a measurable goal, say, "I want to raise $500 for UNICEF to buy school supplies for twenty children."

Whatever way you measure your progress, make sure it is concrete. That means using numbers and deadlines to make sure you can see how much you have done and how much you have left to do. Whether it is marking things on a list or on a calendar, you must be able to see progress. It helps you feel a sense of accomplishment, and it helps motivate you to finish what you have started. For example, make a bar chart or money thermometer to track your progress.

ACHIEVABLE

Any goal that you truly want to reach has to be attainable, which means that you must have the ability, attitudes, skills, financial support and time to make the goal a reality. You are the one who is responsible for whether you reach your goal or not. You may need to stretch yourself a little to reach your goal, but it still needs to be within reach. For example, it may be unrealistic to say you will raise $5,000 in one day. This is probably not attainable. However, if you say "I will raise $1,000 this week," and you achieve it, then you can set the same goal for the next week and know it is attainable. That feeling of success will keep you motivated. As time goes on, the goal that once seemed so far away, maybe even out of reach, is closer than ever and completely attainable.

REALISTIC

Is your goal realistic? Are you willing and able to work toward it? Just because it is a high goal does not mean it isn't realistic. It means that your goal should be something that you can accomplish with the resources and abilities that are available to you. It is a goal that must fit in with your life and with the lives of those who are affected by the goal. But don't forget to stretch yourself. Don't make it too easy. You want to be highly motivated, and that comes more often with big goals than small ones. An example of a realistic goal is wanting to help a community of HIV/AIDS children go to school for a year. An unrealistic goal is wanting to eradicate HIV/AIDS in children. Keep your perspective.

TIMELY

Someday is no day. You must have a time frame for your goal. Set a finish date—a real, solid date by which you will have reached your goal. You can always change the date if you need to, but have it as something to work toward. Having a set date brings your goal to your subconscious mind, making it a reality. Not only should you have an end date, but when you have that date, then you can break your goal down into manageable pieces. It is not enough to say, "I want to raise $5,000 this summer." You need to say, "I will raise $5,000 by August 30, and I will break it down like this." Then set the dates for each $500 or $1,000 that you raise. This will give you a clear attainable target. A time line creates a feeling of urgency—it must be done NOW. And if you find you cannot meet the deadline, you can still move the date. It is not carved in stone. It simply means that you have to alter your plan slightly, but you still set another firm date.

A big check for the Canada Kids Earthquake Challenge

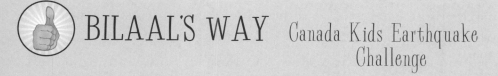

BILAAL'S WAY Canada Kids Earthquake Challenge

The Canada Kids Earthquake Challenge was a challenge I started for UNICEF after a tsunami devastated much of the coastal population in South and Southeast Asia in 2004. Tsunami was a new word to me, but I quickly learned that it is a very powerful and destructive tidal wave.

We were driving home from Niagara Falls on December 26, 2004. I was just going to sleep when I heard the news on the car radio about a huge tidal wave that had caused great damage in Thailand. As I fell asleep, I was thinking about the tsunami and wondering what I should do. I did not have any clear idea at that moment, but I was confident that I would be able to help in some way. When you really want to do something, you will find a way.

When I woke the next morning, I immediately remembered what I had heard the previous night. The papers were full of what had happened. I talked about a plan of action with my parents. They were a bit doubtful, only because I had been really busy for the past couple of months fundraising for Haitian hurricane relief and kids living with HIV/AIDS. We actively discussed the idea for about fifteen minutes. Then I finally said, "Either I stay here and work with my brain, or I go there and work with my hands." I guess that settled it for them. They know that when I make up my mind to do something, nothing will stop me. Besides, they wanted to help the people affected by the tsunami too.

By that point, I knew what I was going to do. I contacted UNICEF to issue the Canada Kids Earthquake Challenge. I already had a contact in Toronto, a woman named Nicole Ireland, who had been involved with the Haiti hurricane appeal. When we met, we discussed what should be done and how much money we should set as the goal. Nicole felt that each child who joined the challenge should raise $10 for the cause. I thought that was too little, and I insisted on $100. Nicole finally said, "Okay. We will support you if that is what you want." She knew that I had faith in Canadian children. The challenge was announced at UNICEF Canada's head office in Toronto. David Agnew, the then-CEO of UNICEF Canada, was there, and I give a speech about the plan, which was very simple. My public announcement and the press release that followed urged each and every child across Canada to raise at least $100, with a final goal of $1,000,000. My mom and the UNICEF people were a little nervous because the goal was so high, but I always believed it would happen.

I thought about what my personal goal for the challenge should be. Once I had set it as $10,000, I spent all that day calling people I knew and asking them to donate. I used the same approach for each and every person I called—I asked them to help children in need. I called uncles, aunts, people I knew from jamatkhana, companies, business owners, schoolteachers, my school principal. You will be surprised how willing people are to help: All you have to do is ask. Have confidence when you are fundraising. One family actually donated $5,000, and they have been my supporters ever since. As soon as I got one big supporter, my confidence skyrocketed, and I was able to contact more people. For the challenge, I ended up personally raising $50,000. The government of Canada was also involved in helping the victims of the tsunami. It agreed to match, dollar for dollar, the money raised up to a certain point. This meant that every dollar we collected would be worth two.

I also approached the Indonesian and Sri Lankan communities in Toronto to get them started doing something to help. When I told them my story, they realized I could really help even though I was so young. The Indonesian community donated to UNICEF, and also organized a huge and successful fundraising dinner event.

I raised most of the money for UNICEF online. UNICEF had set up a page for the Canada Kids Earthquake Challenge on their website. People wishing to donate could go there and contribute. I also set up an online donation account on my organization's website (www.bilaalrajan.com). It is good to have more than one collection point. There are also websites such as www.canadahelps.org and www.tidescanada.org that process donations for charities.

The Canada Kids Earthquake Challenge was helped tremendously by the Toronto District School Board. I was invited to start the ball rolling by giving a speech about the challenge at a Toronto school to about six hundred students. Ten days later, someone from the board called and asked me and David Agnew to come to Valley Park School to receive a check. I was really surprised, because the challenge had been on for such a short period of time. What surprised me and David even more was that in ten days—just ten days—the Toronto District School Board had raised $1.3 million. This was from their own fundraising, and did not include the matching government funds.

The challenge's goal had already been met and passed, but the fundraising was not over. One small boy came to the UNICEF office with the contribution he had collected. It wasn't $100, though. On his own, he had collected $300.

In the end, we raised many millions instead of just one million. Pretty SMART!

With students at King's Edgehill School, Windsor, Nova Scotia

CHAPTER 4

Strength in Numbers

There is always strength in numbers. The more individuals or organizations that you can rally to your cause, the better.
—MARK SHIELDS, JOURNALIST, COLUMNIST AND AUTHOR

D o you ever feel like things would be easier if you could just do them yourself? Doing a project at school would be easier if you could do it alone, right? No one else to worry about. Sometimes this might actually be true, but often it isn't. There is one very important thing you must remember—we do not live alone. Every day we are in constant communication with others. We have to work with others all the time.

Think about it. In my family, we have to work together to ensure that our household runs smoothly. Ideally this is a consistent ongoing exercise in working as a team. That's what this is all about. Teamwork! There is an old saying, "There is no I in the word team." When we work together as a team, no one acts alone and no one should ever have to. Your mom and dad should not be the only ones to wash the dishes, do the laundry, clean the bathrooms and vacuum the floors, when you contribute to the mess as well.

Here is probably the best reason to work with others and why there is strength in doing so. Each and every one of us possesses differences and unique abilities. Celebrate these! They are what make us special, and they are also what makes having a team of people to work with so amazing.

When you work with a group of diverse people you have the perfect opportunity to learn in so many ways. First of all, you learn the valuable lesson that there is more than one way to do something. So many people grow up never learning this lesson or not learning it very well. Not only do you get to see different ways of doing things, but you get to learn from others' experiences. Everyone has different life experiences, and everyone sees the world in a different way. These unique experiences and outlooks allow each person to approach a problem in a different way and come up with unique solutions. Many times, when working on a big project, one person can come up with a solution to a problem where others cannot. In this way, the work can get done efficiently and effectively.

Strength in numbers also comes from the fact that different people are good at different things or have unique strengths and talents. Say you are working on a big science project that includes both a functional model of a volcano and a written report. One person might be good at visualizing and drawing and can draw up a plan. Another person might be more suited to the actual technical act of building the model. The third person in the group may be a good writer and will be able to write an excellent report. Of course, each person participates in each part of the project, but with each person focusing on the part that complements his or her strengths, the project gets completed smoothly and on time. Try to imagine working on this project on your own if you were good at writing, but not as good at building the model. What would the final product be like? Would you have had as much fun? Would you get as good a grade?

Of course, when you work with others there are bound to be disagreements. While these are never fun, they are always an opportunity to learn and grow as a person. First of all, you will learn good communication and conflict-resolution skills when you have to work things out with another person. You will also learn that sometimes you have to go with what the group decides even when you do not agree. Each person has a different point of view, and everyone's opinion matters. Working with others will help you keep an open mind, which is a big advantage when you become an adult.

You can take the idea of strength in numbers and apply it to fundraising and humanitarian efforts as well. While you can raise $100 by yourself, you can raise thousands when you recruit others to help you.

A group of people also has a louder voice than just one person alone. Many people have no way of making their voices heard, so it is often necessary to have a strong voice when speaking on behalf of others. You can do that better with a group of people. When I was fundraising for the hurricanes in Haiti in 2004, I recruited twelve friends to help me sell boxes of cookies. Together we sold over a thousand boxes in less than a week. I know I could never have accomplished that myself.

Working with others is not always easy, but it is always worth it and always rewarding. After all, how boring would the world be if everyone was the same? Something that is created with a team effort is bound to be amazing and the effort worthwhile. For more help with teambuilding, please read and do the exercises for Principle Five, page 111.

When it came to selling cookies as a fundraiser, it made sense to have a team of people. I came up with the idea of starting a team because I have always found that you can accomplish a lot more as a group than by yourself. Think about it this way. If you fundraise alone, you probably know fifty people who might donate to your cause. If you go out and find fifty NEW people, you now have a hundred people who might donate. But suppose you put together a team of ten people—that's a thousand possible donors!

By yourself: 50 people you already know

\+

50 new people

TOTAL = 100 possible donors

10-person Team: 10 × 50 people your team already knows = 500

\+

10 × 50 new people = 500

TOTAL = 1,000 possible donors

If each donation averages $10, then you will raise $9,000 more with a team than on your own. Now do you believe that getting a team organized is worth it?

BILAAL'S WAY The World Partnership Walk

Every year on the last Sunday in May, the Aga Khan Foundation Canada (www.akfc.ca) of the Aga Khan Development Network (www.akdn.org) organizes the World Partnership Walk (www.worldpartnershipwalk.com) in many major cities across Canada. The AKDN is an international network of organizations dedicated to helping people in developing countries. The Walk's aim is to eliminate global poverty by raising funds for people of all ages, no matter what their origins or faith. One hundred percent of the money raised from the Walk goes directly to the people in need.

The Walk is a volunteer-run event that usually takes about an hour and a half. It's a fun thing to do because everyone is cheerful, and there is a good sense of community. The walkers have been sponsored by other individuals or by local businesses. Most sponsors pay the walker a flat rate, but some pay a certain amount for every kilometer covered. All age groups are involved in the Walk—everyone from babies in strollers to seniors in wheelchairs.

E-mail is a tool you must understand and use if you are asking for donations. In the summer of 2007, I was able to raise $5,000 for the World Partnership Walk by sending out just two mass e-mails. I did the same thing for UNICEF's trick-or-treat campaign and was able to bring in lots of donations online. The key is to keep a full and up-to-date e-mail address list at all times. If you have a donor list, it makes things so much easier when you want to contact people. You can simply send one e-mail to as many people as you want and wait for the responses. In this busy world, you will find that some people are more connected through their e-mail than they are through their phone, so sending out e-mails may work to your advantage.

Many people do the Walk as individuals. However, I prefer to have a team of ten or eleven people in the Walk. The members change from year to year, and it takes a bit of organizing, but it is worth it. You have to gather the people, and I usually send e-mails to recruit the members.

We make T-shirts for the walk and get sponsors, which can be very effective. My team raised about $17,000 in total one year!

If you have a team, it gets more kids involved and active; it means there is more awareness about the Walk (or whatever your cause is), and so more money is raised. My motto is, "Together We Can Make a Difference." I truly believe that together we can change the world. We can make a difference in the lives of those who really need our help.

Call in the Big Donors

As we have seen, individual people can make a huge impact in your fundraising. When you collect donations from a large number of people, you can raise a lot of money, even thousands of dollars. But, if you can get big corporations on board, you can do so much more. It's easy to think that big organizations don't have much to do with ordinary people and their everyday lives. Corporations are big—maybe too big— so we don't connect with them. However, there can be advantages to having a connection with a big organization or with more than one at the same time.

Why would big corporations donate to your cause? One of the biggest reasons is because they could receive good publicity. People will see them as community-oriented companies. It is basically free advertising for them. Hopefully that is not the only reason for their contribution, but it is a start. Many companies donate because they truly want to make a positive impact in the world. They want to help those in need and recognize that they are in a position to do so. They also are able to influence others to donate as well, and this can start a chain reaction.

When you are connected to a big corporation, they can advertise for you in their corporate newsletters and at events. By connecting with a corporate donor, you will find that you can significantly increase the number of people you reach. The other advantage to corporate donors is that they may be able to give you material goods for your cause. Even if your goal is to raise money, this money often goes toward buying food, clothing, medicine, building supplies and other essential items. Sometimes big corporations would rather donate goods and services than money, but it all goes to people who need help.

So how do you get those big corporate donors? You have to be confident and just go for it. A corporation is no different than an individual person, maybe just harder to get hold of sometimes. The worst a corporate donor can do is say no. My advice with corporations is not to waste time. Use the Internet to find out the name and number of the head of the company—the CEO—and call him or her directly. You will very likely get this person's secretary, but just ask to leave a message, preferably on voice mail. Then wait for a response. They may call you, but it is more likely that they will call the organization you are raising funds for. You will be amazed at what you can achieve by approaching companies.

With Jim Herder, former Director of Advancement, signing off on an endowment fund for a scholarship at Bilaal's school, St. Andrew's College. The scholarship will be given annually to the graduating middle school student who has performed the most community service that year.

BILAAL'S WAY Hurricane in Haiti (Part I)

Near the end of September 2004, Hurricane Jeanne's heavy rains caused severe flooding and mudslides in Haiti. The damage affected about 80,000 of the 100,000 people in the city of Gonaïves. Imagine what it would be like if a storm caused problems for eighty percent of the people in your town or city. I thought the aid the Haitians were getting was not enough. So I decided to ask for corporate donations. You see the names of companies at sports events, in billboard advertisements and in magazines. If they can support a sports team, they can also support children in need.

I met with the Haitian consular general to find out what sorts of supplies were most important at that time, so I could contact different companies who might provide what was needed. The consular general told me that the main things needed were medicine and food.

First I approached Apotex, a major pharmaceutical company, and they donated almost half a million dollars of medicine. Heinz donated about $50,000 worth of baby food. I contacted seventeen different companies, some by letter and some by calling up the CEO. Almost all of them replied to my letter requesting aid, but not many actually donated. It's still a good idea, though, to make company requests. Once you have a connection with someone, you can ask them again, and that may work. It can be difficult to approach the heads of companies if you don't know them, but if there is somebody in the company that you do know, that person can ask someone higher up. That is another way to have success.

Selling cookies for hurricane-devastated Haiti

CHAPTER 5

Don't Take No for an Answer

Just don't give up trying to do what you really want to do. Where
there is love and inspiration, I don't think you can go wrong.

**—ELLA FITZGERALD, "FIRST LADY OF SONG"
AND ONE OF THE GREATEST JAZZ VOCALISTS OF ALL TIME**

It's Nothing Personal

No matter what kind of fundraising you are doing, many people will say
no to you. This can be very disheartening. The very first thing you need
to understand is that their refusal is not directed at you personally. If
you take people's negative responses to heart, you will want to give up
after the first couple of times it happens. When people say no, they are
saying no to the opportunity to donate. They are not saying no to you.
Fundraising is much like sales. In the sales world, it is commonly known
that it takes ten NOs to get a YES. When you look at it this way, it can
help to think of every NO as being one NO closer to your next YES.

Did you know that the most common reason people give for not
making a donation is simply that they were not asked? This means that
you MUST get out there and ask everyone you can think of. While this
will mean getting more NOs, it will also result in more YES's. Another
thing that will help you avoid a few NOs is to make it personal when you
ask people to donate. If you are raising funds for homeless children, and
you approach a mother playing with her kids in a park, ask her what she
thinks it would be like to have children and be homeless. She is more
likely to give to your cause because you personalized it. It also helps to

give them donation options, if they are available. If someone wants a tax receipt, make sure it is available, even if you can't give it directly. Register your charity with a charitable agency, such as the United Way, or go online to websites such as canadahelps.org. Make sure your charity is listed, and then people can go online to donate to your cause and get a tax receipt.

You will not only get negative responses from individuals who decide not to support your cause. You may also experience negativity on a greater level. For example, finding venues at which to raise funds or sell your fundraising goods can be a challenge. Many venues do not allow solicitation on their property. You have to ask for permission, and you may have to compromise a bit in order to make use of their space. The following story demonstrates how a NO can be turned into a YES, with a little persistence.

 # BILAAL'S WAY Hurricane in Haiti (Part II)

UNICEF wanted to help the victims of the hurricane in Haiti, so they made a plea for help. I was inspired by a photograph in a newspaper of a Haitian child with tears in her eyes. I still remember that photograph as clearly as I did the first day I saw it. It made me realize again that there are children out there who are not as fortunate as I am.

My immediate reaction was to help. My parents suggested donating my allowance. At that time my allowance was ten dollars a month. I said no, not because I didn't want to donate my allowance, but because it was not enough. I thought about what I could do and remembered that my dad sold boxes of cookies at his business. His business is called Good Foods Enterprises (www.goodfoods.ca) and it specializes in supplying healthy and nutritious foods to educational institutions across Ontario. He agreed to donate a few boxes of cookies so I could sell them, expecting me to sell only about twenty or thirty boxes.

I went to school the next day, and I asked my principal, Mr. Harry Giles, if I could sell boxes of cookies at recess for this cause. He didn't know what to say because the school had never been asked anything like this before. He said he needed to talk to his vice-principal. Twenty-four hours later, I still had not received a response, so I followed up and finally got my answer. Mr. Giles said no to the morning and afternoon recesses, but he gave me permission to sell at lunchtime. For the first little while, there wasn't much activity. Not many students were receptive, but I didn't give up. I decided that I'd give away samples of the cookies. It was a good move, because after the sampling, there were a lot more sales. Some people even bought four boxes at one lunch recess! Eventually I was allowed to sell at all the recesses. A lot of students were happy to donate because they wanted the cookies, but it was really good to see that at least some of them supported the cause because they understood the issues.

I didn't meet any objections while I was selling cookies on my own at school, but it was a different story when I tried to raise funds with my team at popular spots in Toronto. We couldn't collect in Union Station, because it was too crowded; we were asked to go outside. The security people also asked us not to hang around together as a large group (there were thirteen of us), so we had to split up into groups of two or three. Even though we had some obstacles to overcome, we raised close to $6,500 for the children of Haiti.

Never Give Up

The writer Jack London said, "You can't wait for inspiration. You have to go after it with a club." Okay, you don't have to go out fundraising with a club over your shoulder. If you want to fundraise but you are meeting with objections, don't give up; just keep on trying. Giving up is never the answer to anything. If you are a fundraiser and you are dealing with people who are unresponsive, keep on trying—but with different people. Don't get stuck on one negative comment. There are always more people out there that you can count on, people who are happy to donate.

If you are a fundraiser and you're talking with someone who is undecided about whether to give, sometimes it helps to ask for a quick yes or no answer. Then, no matter what they say, just move on. Remember, you are acting for your cause. It's not personal. There are a lot of wonderful people in this world, and they are very supportive. Some people say that they do not have money at that moment, and that they will come back later—and they do! When I was raising funds selling cookies at Harbourfront in Toronto, I met a man who said he didn't have money but would be back. I was doubtful he would come back, but two hours later, he came back to buy not one but five boxes, because he couldn't get me out of his mind. If you are going to raise funds, you have to use your imagination and contact all sorts of people who might help. If you have an idea, follow it through. You may not meet with success every time, but that doesn't matter. With every step you take, you come closer to your goal.

Avoiding No by Establishing Rapport

One way to avoid getting rejected is to learn how to establish rapport with the person you are asking for a donation. Rapport simply means that you have a good relationship with that person and can connect with him or her on a personal level. There are some people who are able to talk with others easily. They can tell a story and make people laugh and relate to them in a special way, right from the beginning. However, many of us cannot do that, but we can still establish a rapport. We can listen and look and ask questions in order to determine how someone learns. By listening to the types of words someone uses, you can figure out what types of words to use when talking about your cause. For example, you can ask someone how their weekend was or what their favorite toy was as a child. Then listen for the words they use. Do they tend to use visual (seeing) words, audio (hearing) words or kinesthetic words (words that have to do with touch)? Mariaemma Willis and Victoria Kindle Hodson give a great explanation of learning style in their book, *Discover Your Child's Learning Style*.

For example, three people go for a walk in the woods and sit by a beautiful stream. When describing it, the visual person says the stream looks like a blue ribbon, the audio person talks about the babbling brook and the kinesthetic person talks about how the stream tickles her toes. When you get used to the types of words a person uses, then you can talk about your fundraising idea using the same types of words. The person will be more likely to relate to you and give accordingly.

It also helps to establish rapport by mirroring the person you are talking to. Pay attention to gestures, speech patterns, mannerisms and the way people move. Also learn to ask open-ended questions, which are questions that have to be answered with more than a simple yes or no. Also, you can ask any question that requires a description.

You also need to listen closely and give the person you are talking to your complete attention. If you are staring out the window while they are speaking or if you are fidgeting, making notes or interrupting them, you are sending the message that they are not important. The person you are speaking with needs to know that they have your complete attention, and that it is not only about their donation.

All these techniques put together are called active listening. Of course, it will take you time and effort to develop your active listening skills. You can use the exercises in Principle Three (page 102) to help you. Practice on your family and friends, but don't tell them what you are doing. That way, you will get their honest response. Does this mean that everyone will say yes to you? No. But it will increase the YES's and help you make valuable connections.

With Ben Mulroney

CHAPTER 6

Media Makes the Difference

I respect very much the role of the media in our society;
I think they can be very, very helpful.

**—ALBERTO GONZALES, THE FIRST HISPANIC TO SERVE
AS THE UNITED STATES ATTORNEY GENERAL**

I n the previous chapter I discussed how teamwork makes fundraising more effective. Well, the media—television, radio, newspapers and the Internet—can also make a difference and really help us get better results. They can be a part of our team if we make use of them. There is a lot of generosity and kindness in the world, even in big corporations. You just have to be honest and genuine with everyone, from a CEO to your next-door neighbor, and have confidence in what you are doing.

Mass media is the fastest, easiest and cheapest way to get the word out about your fundraising efforts. If you are holding an event or a sale of some kind, the local media will generally list it or announce it for free. Radio stations are a great way to get the word out. They are generally very involved in the community and will announce special events daily. Your local TV news station may also do the same thing and may even interview you. The same goes for the local newspaper. It is often quite easy to get the local newspaper to interview you and write an article about what you are doing and where people can find you. With this type of exposure, numerous things can happen:

1. People who would not have known about your cause will be able to find you and will come out and support you.

2. People who cannot get out to see or meet you will still be aware of the cause and will support you.
3. People who see you may be so interested and inspired by you that they may join you or begin a fundraising campaign of their own.

There was a lot of media interest when I was in the tsunami-affected countries. I did a *Toronto Star* interview on the phone from the Maldives. My story was also picked up by the Associated Press and broadcast worldwide. My grandmother lives in Calgary, and she called us in the Maldives to say that she had seen me on television.

I did an interview in Thailand and a live interview on CBC, as well as interviews for local channels in various countries. UNICEF arranged an interview at a hotel. There were lots of TV channels represented, and the lobby was full. People were amazed at all the activity. I was able to explain a bit about why I was there, and the audience was interested in what made me get involved in the first place.

This media attention worked so well that Jamieson, a vitamin company, called me up while I was in Indonesia. They had seen me in the media, and they wanted to donate. They shipped $153,000' worth of vitamins and health products to Indonesia, which made a terrific difference in the lives of many Indonesians after the tsunami.

The prime minister of Canada in 2004 was Paul Martin, who had met with Bono, the lead singer of the band U2, to talk about raising funds for famine relief in Africa. Mr. Martin was obviously open to the idea of fundraising. I had a call one night from UNICEF telling me that I was going to meet the prime minister. We were going to talk about fundraising in general, and about my fundraising efforts on behalf of the tsunami victims in Southeast Asia and the hurricane victims in Haiti. This happened just after I had made the acrylic plates for HIV/AIDS fundraising, so I gave him a plate I had made that had the Canadian flag on it. Media from around the world covered our meeting, and a lot more donations came in afterward.

Sometimes celebrities will lend their names and popularity to a good cause. For example, the Canada For Asia concert was organized and broadcast by the CBC in January 2005. I had already had interviews with CBC radio and CBC television about the Canada Kids Earthquake Challenge, which was great publicity. They must have been impressed with my interviews, because they decided they wanted to put me on the Canada For Asia concert. The event took place in a couple of CBC studios. There were different musicians in each room, and it was quite a relaxed atmosphere, with chairs placed here and there so people could sit and watch the show. Celebrities performed, and the show was broadcast live on television so viewers could call in and donate. Over the course of five to seven hours about $4 million was raised through telephone donations. It was an interesting evening, and I met many celebrities, from Olympic athletes to astronauts, authors, hat and clothing designers and famous musicians.

I was given this opportunity since I was already very involved in the tsunami fundraising efforts and raising awareness of the situation. When you are authentic in your message, the media and everyone around will pick up on it. You don't need a big concert to promote your message, just a big heart and hard work!

Meeting the media

BILAAL'S WAY National UNICEF Day

Most people probably know that UNICEF is an organization that helps children all over the world. David Miller, who was mayor of Toronto in 2004, proclaimed October 31 National UNICEF Day, and I was able to promote the event at my school. Then I had my first front-page newspaper interview.

I was really nervous about being interviewed, but it helped to know that I was raising awareness to assist children halfway across the world, and that they would be better off because of it. The *Toronto Star*, the *Toronto Sun* and a number of Chinese newspapers reported on the proclamation. The publicity really helped the fundraising. When people know what to expect, they are often more willing to give. One lady told me that she'd found out where we were going to be selling cookies because of seeing me on TV. She bought two cookie boxes and also gave me a $5 donation that she said was from her mom.

Even if you can't get on TV, try your local newspaper or radio station—you'll be amazed how much it can help!

CHAPTER 7

Public Speaking

There are three things to aim at in public speaking: first,
to get into your subject, then to get your subject into yourself,
and lastly, to get your subject into the heart of your audience.
—ALEXANDER GREGG, EPISCOPALIAN CLERGYMAN AND BISHOP OF TEXAS

W hen you become involved in fundraising, you may have to speak
to groups of people. It might be a small group, such as your class
at school, or a large group, such as an entire school assembly
or a TV audience. A lot of people find the idea of public speaking quite
frightening, but it does not have to be that way.

I have had to talk to audiences of all ages. It is a great opportunity
to tell people about the good they can do, as well as about the good they
have already done. I have spoken to groups across Canada as well as in
cities in the United States and on my international travels. I have been a
keynote speaker at conferences and have presented my message at high
school symposiums. I was invited to be a keynote speaker in Dallas,
Texas, at a dinner where volunteers were receiving awards for their
contributions. The next morning, I gave a presentation to the children
and parents of the Ismaili congregation in Dallas. At the dinner, the
master of ceremonies told the audience about the activities I had been
involved in, how much money I had raised and so on, so the audience
knew a bit about why I was there. Then it was my turn to speak.

I don't like prepared speeches, but I do like public speaking. I'll have
a few points in my head that I want to make, and I just start talking.
It's easy if you speak from the heart, even if you feel nervous in the

beginning. I told the audience in Dallas about what I had seen on my travels, about how I got started with fundraising. I related some of my experiences and told them my motto, *Together We Can Make a Difference.* I spoke for about twenty minutes, and the audience really enjoyed what I had to say. They stood up and cheered. After I spoke at the morning session, I answered questions for about an hour and a half.

If you speak from the heart and show people how to make a difference in other people's lives, that's all you need to do. Public speaking gives me the chance to get people excited about helping those in need. It's still the personal touch that is important—it's just to a bigger audience.

I have also done some public speaking in the countries that needed our help. Here the message is different. I'm not trying to raise money. I am trying to bring hope. I let people know that there are other people in the world who care about them. I also want them to know that if they can believe in themselves and take action to be the best they can be, then that will make things even better. Sometimes I meet kids who ask me how I raised money, because they are looking for ways to start fundraising in their own communities.

Some kids I spoke with in Malawi shared that they lost their parents to HIV/AIDS, and that they were now taking care of their grandparents or living with relatives. When I asked them to tell me the one thing they wanted the most, they said, "Food." The second most common answer? A soccer ball. I was able to tell them that food was on its way, and that I would work on getting them soccer balls. Public speaking can be a two-way street—just don't be too afraid to try.

Open Your Mouth—and Your Heart

Here are a few tips on public speaking that might help if you are feeling nervous or unsure of yourself.

1. The audience wants to hear what you have to say. They are very interested. Focus on them and on your message instead of focusing on yourself.

2. Ensure that your message is right for your audience. Even though you may speak about the same things to adults and kids, you will find that you relate to them in different ways and with different examples and stories.

3. Do not rush. Instead of speaking word-for-word from a prepared speech, pretend you are talking with your friends or your parents and just speak from the heart.

4. Move around naturally. You do not have to be stuck behind a podium for the whole thing. Use your regular gestures and mannerisms.

5. Keep things short and to the point. You need to know how long your speech is supposed to be. If you are speaking to kids, you may need to keep it shorter than if you are talking to adults.

6. Always make eye contact with your audience. This will help you connect with them and get them involved. They will be more inclined to pay attention and acknowledge what you are saying.

7. Make sure you practice your speech or your speech points before the big day.

8. Always be available to answer questions after your speech. People will want to know more and talk with you one-on-one.

9. If someone disagrees with something that you have said, discuss it with him or her after your speech is over. Remember that they have every right to express their opinion, even if you do not agree with it.

10. Have fun! Make it personal and enjoy what you are doing.

What is truly important to me is spreading the message. Sure I can work hard to raise much-needed money, and we have already discussed how effective it is to have many people working toward a cause. While I still fundraise as much as possible, I feel it is even more effective to educate and inspire others to do the same. I have talked to a lot of Canadian kids, some through events organized by schools and teachers' boards who contact UNICEF, and some who contact me or my parents through my organization (www.bilaalrajan.com). The presentations usually take place in schools, and I have talked about everything from my own story to the plight of children in other parts of the world. I usually have a few points I want to make, and then I just talk about what I saw and how people are getting help or about what they still need.

Talking like this means that the message of helping those in real need can be spread to many who can help. Members of the audience often ask questions, and they can be encouraged to take action. Those who have already donated are happy to know that their money has greatly helped the lives of others.

I have made several computer slideshow presentations for talks in schools. That way, the audience can see what it is really like for people halfway across the world who need our help. Usually the audience asks questions about life in developing countries: what kinds of houses the people live in or how they get water or medical attention. They sometimes ask if I go to school or skip classes, and how I am doing at school. I'm happy to say that I do go to school, enjoy classes and get very good grades (being an "A" student is also hard work). So it is possible to do fundraising and homework too.

CHAPTER 8

Other Ways to Give

If you want happiness for an hour, take a nap.
If you want happiness for a day, go fishing.
If you want happiness for a year, inherit a fortune.
If you want happiness for a lifetime, help somebody.
—CHINESE PROVERB

Throughout this book I have spoken about raising money. However, there are other ways you can help, once you have found something you are passionate about. As I said before, not all help comes in the form of money. Here are just a few examples.

- Volunteer in the local soup kitchen
- Run a food drive for the local food bank
- Run a clothing drive for a local charity
- Volunteer in a senior citizen's home
- Volunteer in your local library
- Volunteer at your local humane society, or take in foster pets or strays
- Collect books to send to Africa or other countries
- Collect goods to send to people in need around the world
- Write letters to officials asking for help for those in need
- Travel somewhere where you can volunteer to help those in need
- Donate money and/or time to worthy causes

You can even volunteer to help a classmate with his schoolwork, if you feel that is important. It is all about personal choice. As I said before, just make sure it is something you feel passionately about. I like to work with UNICEF because it helps children. You may prefer another charity, and I don't think it matters which one. It is the helping that is the good thing.

 # BILAAL'S WAY Vacations With a Purpose

BUILDING HOUSES IN HAWAII

We, as a family, made a decision a few years ago to take vacations with a purpose, and so each year we volunteer and donate our time during our vacations. A lot of my friends think this is an odd thing to do on vacation, but I firmly believe that as we get to know more about other people in other places, we are living my motto, "Together We Can Make A Difference."

In the summer of 2006, while vacationing in Hawaii, I was able to work with an organization called Habitat for Humanity, which builds houses for the underprivileged. The organization began in 1976 in Americus, Georgia, when a group of people who were in need of housing got together with volunteers to help each other build homes. They now work in ninety countries around the world and have created homes for 225,000 families who would otherwise be left on the street or in inadequate housing. Talk about making a difference together.

LIGHTING UP MEXICO

For about four years, my family and I spent some time in Mexico. We usually went to a village called El Coyote, in the state of Oaxaca, just outside Huatulco. I got to know a boy named Mario from the local village, and we became good friends even though I did not know Spanish, and he spoke no English; we learnt fast. He told me that it was hard to do his homework because when he was studying at night he had to use a kerosene lamp, which was dangerous. The fumes affected his eyes and his throat, making it hard to concentrate.

I felt badly for him, and I wanted to help. I did some research and found out that LED lights might be the solution. So when I got home, I did a science experiment and entered it as a presentation for the science fair in my school. I tested LED lights to see if they were more economical over a five-year period when compared to battery-powered flashlights or kerosene lamps. LED lights turned out to be the most efficient system.

When we went back to Mexico the next summer, I bought some lights and solar panels with money from my savings and took them with me. We were driving to Mexico from Ontario, Canada, and thought we might have problems at the border or with customs, but everything went well. When we got to the village, we were able to put in the solar panels, which ran the LED lights. They were a great success. I was glad that I had been able to help, and I hoped the LED lights would mean the children could get their homework done easily—and that the lights would be useful for other things too. That was the start of my LED light project, which has lit up a lot of houses in rural villages.

TANZANIA—HIV/AIDS EDUCATION

In the summer of 2007, we went to Tanzania to volunteer. I taught HIV/AIDS education, awareness and prevention to people in the area. I spent a lot of time in the Tangeru region and had a great time imparting the knowledge. People were very supportive and learned a lot. Due to the language barrier, I had a translator named John. I also gave my empowerment workshops and spoke in a lot of schools in different communities. I was able to visit and spend time at orphanages—and this is what really moved me—seeing all those children without parents. I can't imagine not having my mom and dad. These children were orphaned because their parents had died of HIV/AIDS, or they were simply dumped into garbage bins because their parents did not want them.

The conditions they lived in were unbelievable. There were fifteen orphans to one room, three orphans sharing one bunk bed. Can you see yourself sharing a bunk bed with two other people? They were all squished together up in that little bed, and all the clothing that they owned fit in a grocery bag. Here in North America, we are always looking for the next cool thing—a new video game, a new pair of shoes, a new CD, a new skateboard. These kids don't have all those material things, but they seem joyful just the same.

There was one child who I remember very clearly. His name was David, and he was found on the steps of a hospital and brought to the Samaritan Village Orphanage in Arusha, Tanzania. After I met David, I knew what my new calling was. Here was a child who had been rejected, abandoned and left to fend for himself, but he was still inquiring, playful, wide-eyed and loving! I wanted to help orphans because, due to HIV/AIDS, there are so many of them in this world. So I founded my first nursery school—Hands for Help Nursery School in the rural village of Arusha. There are now seventy-eight orphans attending the school, and my organization is presently supporting that school. I started my own business so that I could support my school from my own funds. My business is one of inspiring others by doing seminars, coaching and other related activities so that I will have enough money to pay for this school and help orphans all around the world. In Tanzania I met a wonderful lady named Mama Elizabeth. Her calling is to look after orphans and women. She consults with NGOs (Non-Governmental Organizations) and provides HIV/AIDS education. She also gives half her salary to educate and empower women with financial information and a whole host of other skills. She is my partner in this worthy cause, and together we are going to make a big difference.

I know I have given you a lot of information about fundraising and about how to get involved in raising support and awareness for a cause that you believe in. Do you feel overwhelmed by it all? You're right to be overwhelmed. It's a lot to take on. But as long as you believe you can do it, without any doubt or any fear, then you CAN accomplish your goals.

I have never doubted for a moment that I could achieve my fundraising goals and, as a result, I have not only accomplished them, I have surpassed them. I have also inspired others along the way and that inspiration is continually returning to me. This law—often called the Law of Attraction—is as basic as the law of gravity. It is operating in the universe all of the time. It is based on the concept that thoughts are things. It is true that everything in the universe is made up of the same basic parts. Your body is made up of atoms, and so is the book you are holding. At the most basic level, even things that seem solid to us are really just energy. Of course, I am not going to talk about the physics of it, but I believe that our thoughts are also energy.

When we think something, we send energy out into the universe with that thought. It is kind of like when you turn on a light switch. When you flick the switch, you make energy move into the light bulb. Energy is a real thing, and it makes changes in the physical world.

So how do your thoughts affect your life? Simple. What you think is what happens in your life. If you think you are going to achieve something, you will. As the poet Virgil said, "They can because they think they can." If you do not think you will achieve something, if you are doubtful or afraid, then you won't. The universe sends you more of the same kind of energy that you send out with your thoughts.

Now, it is very hard to control all your thoughts. We have about sixty thousand thoughts every day, and if you tried to keep track of them all you would go crazy! The best way to change how you think is to monitor your feelings. When you feel good, good things happen and when you feel bad, bad things happen. Remember it is called the Law of **Attraction**. You attract into your life whatever you think about. If you think of having less, you'll have less. If you think of having more, you'll have more. At first I wanted to raise $100 to help the hurricane victims of Haiti. After that, I quickly raised it to $500, then $1,000, even though I had only collected $50. The more positive I was that I could achieve more, the more I succeeded. We raised over $6,500!

Making Change

The first and best way to begin your journey of attracting good things into your life is to be grateful. Gratitude is about being happy with what you have instead of wanting what you don't have. It is about choosing what you focus your thoughts on. If you are unhappy because your grades in school are not as high as you would like, then you could feel really bad. You might have thoughts like this:

- I don't understand the material
- I'm frustrated that my best friend gets better marks
- I don't like my teacher
- I'm stressed about the test
- I'm worried that I'll fail
- I should be able to pass the test but I can't
- Why am I having so much trouble?

When you focus on thoughts like these ones, you are not taking responsibility for your own circumstances. Now, instead of focusing on your marks and how badly you feel about them, think of what you have to be grateful for at school. You might be grateful that:

- You have a good school to go to
- You have a really knowledgeable teacher this year
- Your parents are very supportive and helpful when it comes to your schoolwork
- You have lots of great friends at school
- There is an excellent tutoring program after school

You can do this for any and every part of your life. When you wake up each morning, think about what you have to be grateful for that day. Do more than just think about it. FEEL it. Make sure you get your feelings involved so that it means more to you. Do this again before you go to bed. After a while, it will be as easy as breathing.

Another thing you can do is write out a gratitude list, which will keep growing and changing as you grow older. This list can also be as long as you want; there is no limit to gratitude. Just start writing, and anytime you think of something new, add it to the list. Carry your list with you, and, whenever you feel bad feelings coming on, pull out that list and read it. Find things on the list that have to do with what you are finding difficult. Change your bad feelings to good feelings and keep the good energy flowing.

To use the example of grades again, say you have low grades and you feel bad about it. Chances are you think a lot about how bad your grades are. You might think you are being positive by saying, "I know my grades are low, but I will bring them up" or "I really want to improve my grades." However, this is still focusing your thoughts on the negative. You do not want low grades. You want high grades. So think about what you want. Think about high grades! When you focus your thoughts on high grades continuously and passionately, you will achieve high grades. You will send good energy into the universe and it will come back to you.

Apply this to your fundraising or any activity you want to help in. If you are new at this, you may feel nervous and hesitant. If you have done it before but have set a higher goal, you may feel doubtful that you can achieve it. STOP! I want you to imagine that you have already raised the funds you wanted to raise. I want you to imagine you have gone beyond your goal and raised even more money. Keep these thoughts in your mind all the time and it will happen.

Final Tips

Are there people in your life who seem to have it all? They are very successful, and they never seem to have any trouble getting what they want or need. Take a close look at these people. I bet they are very positive people who know what they want and go for it instead of complaining about what they don't have. Here are a final few tips that can help you create that positive outlook in your life.

BE OPTIMISTIC

Being optimistic means seeing the good side of things and feeling sure that things will work out. Complaining is the worst thing you can do. Complaining oozes negative energy and will keep you stuck where you are. When you come at life from an optimistic point of view, you believe things will work out. In fact, you just know they will. Many people who are truly successful never knew how they were going to get there, they just knew they would. The way unfolded before them as they went along.

TAKE RISKS

Do not be afraid to take risks. Risks are what make life truly interesting and they are what allow you to accomplish more. Taking risks is about stepping outside of your comfort zone and going for it! No matter what you do, there will always be risk involved. You take a risk every time you cross the street, and you take a risk every time you decide to go after a goal, but it is worth it because without risks, life would be boring.

SEE THE HELP AROUND YOU

There is always help around you and available to you, if you are willing to see it. Whether this help comes from other people or from your higher power, it is present all of the time. It is your responsibility to seek out and accept the help and use it to make your goals a reality.

CHAPTER 9

Seeing Is Believing

The very air in which you live is an inspiration.
—WILLIAM HENRY MOODY, AMERICAN POLITICIAN, LAWYER AND JUDGE

Where Does the Money Go?

This is such a common question, and it is a good one too. People have the right to know where their hard-earned dollars are going when they donate it to a cause. They want to know they are helping people (or animals or whatever the focus of the cause is), and that the money they donate is paying for far more than administration costs. Not only do they want to know that the money is going directly to the cause, but they also often want a breakdown of how the money is spent. How much went to food or clothing or medicine or clean water or education? These are good questions, and you should make sure you know the answers before you start fundraising.

When the tsunami hit Southeast Asia in December of 2004, I was working hard to raise funds and awareness. Many people are content to ask questions and receive answers. I wanted to see for myself. I got to the point where I wanted to know, firsthand, where the donations were going. I wanted to see the food, medicine, and clean drinking water being shipped to the people. I wanted to see how the people lived and how they had been affected by the tsunami. Most of all, I wanted to see the children and let them know that children all over the world cared about them and were doing their best to help.

In January 2005, I decided that I wanted to go to Southeast Asia in order to see what the money Canadian kids had raised was doing for the victims. I wanted to make sure the money was not being wasted. I begged my parents to take me, and in March 2005 we flew from Toronto to Hong Kong, and then on to Thailand, Sri Lanka, the Maldives and Indonesia. UNICEF members helped us out by arranging car travel in the different locations. They also organized trips to schools and relief programs. I am happy to report that the money donated and collected in Canada was put to excellent use.

THAILAND

In Thailand, I talked with and thanked a lot of volunteers from the UNICEF office there. UNICEF responded quickly to this area after the disaster struck. I visited daycare centers and schools in villages and small towns. I went almost everywhere there were children orphaned by the tsunami. It is hard to believe, but one fishing village with over four thousand families was totally wiped out. Imagine the street where you live and the streets around you just disappearing.

Many of the children had had terrible experiences. At one of the schools, I spoke with one child at length. He told me about seeing his parents and other relatives being washed away, and how he could do nothing to save them. He was helpless to do anything but watch them die.

In a fishing village I visited, I saw a Thai police harbor patrol boat resting against a hill two kilometers inland. It was a very strange sight, but it gave me an idea of how terrifying it must have been during the flooding. I visited a Thai school that had been flooded, and you could see from marks on the walls how high the water had come. Even though this school was three kilometers inland, the stains left behind from the water showed the water level had been higher than my head when I was standing on a chair.

There was destruction everywhere, but the people were incredible. I visited a refugee camp that was funded by UNICEF. There the children expressed their thoughts through paintings called batiks. I was able to see how they went from painting about death and destruction to making calm and peaceful drawings. I bought a few batiks and took one with me to the Focus Humanitarian Assistance conference in Dallas, Texas. I showed it to some of the guests, and it helped them understand how courageous the people in Thailand were. I was stunned that the batik was later auctioned for about $5,000 at the conference, and the money went back to Focus to help others in need.

It's hard to believe that even though these kids had gone through death and destruction three months earlier, they were ready to get on with their normal lives. Their strength and courage were particularly obvious in one of the schools I visited. I say "school," but classes were actually going on in a tent because the school building had been destroyed. Even so, everyone was eager to learn. They were looking to their future, not back at their past. We can all learn something from their spirit.

MALDIVES

After Thailand we visited the Maldives. We landed in the capital, Mali, a very clean and beautiful place. The population is ninety percent Muslim, and you could hear the Koran being recited from the mosques. Again, UNICEF was very helpful. They came to the airport to meet me. Even though I had traveled there not to fundraise, but to see the place and the results of the destruction, UNICEF brought the media with them.

During my time in the Maldives, UNICEF arranged visits to schools, hospitals, and even temporary shelters. It was a busy time, seeing people and talking to them for a few hours at a time, from early in the morning until late at night. There were press conferences, and often kids would be there asking questions and telling their stories.

Some of the shelters I saw were built within only seven days after the tsunami hit in order to give temporary shelter to the survivors. A typical shelter was about the size of a normal bedroom in Canada, so you can imagine how small it was. That space had to house as many as sixteen people.

Gemendhoo is an island in the Maldives. Before the tsunami destroyed their homes, the inhabitants lived a simple and peaceful life. One day I visited Gemendhoo with some children who had lived there. This was their first trip back to their homes in three months. They were very sad because of the destruction caused by the tsunami, and they could not look at the remains. They simply hid their faces in their hands.

In almost all the places I visited where there was a mosque, a temple or a church, these buildings had been barely touched by the tsunami or floodwaters. The person who took me around the island told me that while you would find six or even seven feet of water flooding some houses, there would be only a foot of water in the mosque. I find this extraordinary. Makes you wonder, doesn't it?

During this visit, I was honored to be invited to a private meeting with Maumoon Abdul Gayoom, the president of the Maldives. I wondered why he would want to meet a young kid like me. We met in his office for about an hour and a half. I was there with my parents, the office staff of UNICEF Maldives, and the president's secretarial assistant. It was an interesting meeting, and we discussed why I was in his country and what I had been doing there.

It was a wonderful experience and a great honor to meet the president of the Maldives. I wanted to give him something at the end of our meeting to show my gratitude. I didn't have much with me, but a Canada hat seemed about right. He loved it and thanked me! Little things can mean and say a lot.

SRI LANKA

Nicole Ireland, from the UNICEF office in Canada, was in Sri Lanka, so I felt very comfortable, and she helped us a lot. Parts of Sri Lanka were completely devastated; traveling with the roads washed out and debris everywhere was not easy. Even though it was hard to get around, Nicole was able to set up some visits and get a van to take us to different locations. These trips would sometimes take eight hours.

Galle is a town situated on the southwestern tip of Sri Lanka. It was for many years the main port on the island. But on December 26, 2004, the city was devastated by the tsunami. Thousands were killed.

I saw the remains of a train wreck near Galle that cost two thousand lives. The train had just been in the wrong place at the wrong time. The force of the tsunami had thrown it and its passengers two hundred meters from the track. The locals and the government have left the train there and now treat it as a monument to those who died in the tsunami.

At the train wreck, a little man standing beside the train told me the story of how he had lost everything. He told me as well how he was planning for his future and trying to rebuild his life. I was amazed at how people were getting on with their lives in the middle of such devastation.

Even though many people had lost everything, they still invited us into their shelters and offered us drinks and food. They shared stories of how they watched their homes being washed away. Some of the children spoke of how their parents had disappeared and how they could do nothing to save them.

When I visited schools in Sri Lanka, I found another way that children were healing themselves from the impact of the tsunami. This was through a program of music and play that was funded by UNICEF. I participated in some of it and found it very enjoyable. The activities included making art, playing the drums and having parades. They may be only small activities, but they are easy and fun for children to do. That is important, especially when you have suffered so much. It helped them express feelings that may have been bottled up, feelings they didn't know how to express. It also helped them keep their minds off the horrifying reality of their lives.

INDONESIA

The last place I visited was Indonesia. We landed in Jakarta, and the next day we went by plane to the worst area of devastation—Banda Aceh.

We stayed there for three days. There were restrictions in place, but UNICEF Indonesia arranged a special pass for us to go there. I met Karen Foss from the Canadian Embassy, and she was very helpful and knowledgeable.

This was the region that was hit hardest by the tsunami, and it was horrible. I felt so devastated. Everywhere I looked there was nothing but rubble. It was incredibly disturbing to witness that level of destruction. Most of the buildings were gone; this is where the biggest number of people had to rebuild their lives.

In Banda Aceh, donations were spent on shoes, clothing, water tanks and water purifiers. It's easy for us to go into the kitchen, turn on a tap and get a drink of nice clean water, but the children in Banda Aceh had a much tougher time. Their water supplies were contaminated. Now, after receiving international aid, they could drink clean water.

Money was also spent on necessities like food, temporary shelters, cots and first-aid supplies. Some money went toward new buildings, and some was spent on sports equipment so that the children could have some recreation.

They handled the destruction very creatively in some cases. For example, in Banda Aceh, the power of the tsunami carried a five-hundred-foot coal freighter—that's right, a huge ship—from the water to the middle of a road going through the town. How did the locals deal with this situation? They set up a convenience store and a restaurant in the shade of this ship. How ingenious! The freighter cannot be moved because of its size and weight, so the people turned it into a part of the city.

The Internal Displaced Persons (IDP) camps I visited were also an incredible sight. It was great to see people rebuilding their lives. For example, some had set up shops outside the tents they lived in so they could re-establish a way of life and their own livelihood. The last thing the children of Banda Aceh said to me before I left was, "Please do not forget us," and I would like to humbly request we do not forget these children and all the children around the world who need our help.

MALAWI

Since my visit to the tsunami-affected regions in Southeast Asia, I have been privileged to travel elsewhere. I visited Malawi for two weeks in November 2005. We flew from Toronto to Amsterdam, then to Kenya, and on to Lilongwe in Malawi. I had done some fundraising for HIV/AIDS in 2004, and I had also supported UNICEF's Food For Africa program for trick-or-treating in 2004 and 2005. I wanted to see what Canadian kids' money was doing for children in Malawi and across Africa.

We used a UNICEF car to go to various villages. It was an honor to meet Stonach, our driver, who has since died of HIV/AIDS. No one knew at the time we visited that he was HIV-positive. It made me realize that if we get sick in Canada, we don't mind going to a doctor, but in Africa there is a social stigma attached to having HIV/AIDS. People do not want to admit to others that they are suffering from this disease, so they will not go for help or look for medication even when they so desperately need it. It was devastating to see children who had been orphaned by HIV/AIDS. They were often living with their grandparents, earning money to help keep things going.

In Canada we study math and science and languages. However, in Malawi, HIV/AIDS is such a problem and is so common that in classes at school, kids learn how to treat and help HIV/AIDS victims. The severity of the HIV/AIDS situation in Malawi really struck me when I learned this. These children have to learn about survival in a way we do not. We have space and light in our schools, and we're quite comfortable. In Malawi, there are sometimes three kids to one desk, if they have any desks at all. Most of the time, classes are held outside no matter what the weather is like. The teachers and students write on blackboards built out of brick with a covering of black mud.

When we go to school here in North America, we can bring lunch and snacks with us, or we can go to the school cafeteria and buy a nutritious lunch. Then we go home for dinner. The students I met in Malawi only got one meal a day—porridge that was served at school. The porridge is warm and thick and doughy, and the kids love it, maybe because it is the only food they get. Parents volunteer to do the cooking, and the porridge is made right at school.

In the midst of all this suffering there was still time for football (what we call soccer). This was something else I found hard to believe. The soccer ball they used at schools in Malawi was made out of a pig's bladder and stomach wrapped up in newspaper and plastic bags. That was what they kicked around. After I had given out all the soccer balls that we had brought with us (they had *Canada* written on them), there wasn't much I could do for these other children. I decided right there to help out, and later I was able to buy all the schools I visited a good soccer ball. They were relatively cheap (about $7 per ball), but unaffordable for the children there. The smiles and laughter were well worth the price I paid.

Most of the families in Malawi do not have clean running water or much access to food. They live in small brick houses. The older kids took care of the younger ones. For example, I visited three girls who were living on their own in a very small brick house about the size of a washroom. In most first-world countries, parents look after their children. They feed and clothe them and take care of them for many years. In Malawi, what I found really astounding was that even at the age of ten or twelve, a child would often be in charge of the household. He or she would have to house everybody and take care of grandparents and younger siblings. They worked as well, barely having time to go to school, if they were able to go to school at all.

You are not going to believe this next part. When you go to a mall in Canada or the US, you see clothing shops, grocery stores and specialty stores. You also see lots of coffee shops. In Malawi, it just blew me away that there were—not *coffee* shops, but *coffin* shops everywhere. Can you imagine this? So many people are dying of HIV/AIDS in Malawi that it is normal to have a coffin shop on every corner. Seeing the coffin shops made me want to do even more to help children in Africa.

This Is Just the Beginning

It is my wish that you come away from reading this book with a clear vision of what you want to do to help others. It is an even greater wish that you come away **knowing** that you can help others in any way you want, and that you can **do anything** you want to do, just by using the Law of Attraction in your life. Just discover your passion and then follow it and believe. The rest will come.

Even if I motivate only one person out of fifty thousand with my talks, I am still happy. It is one drop in the ocean, and every drop counts. It is the same with this book. If just one person who reads this book becomes inspired to reach his or her goal, then I have accomplished my goal, and I am happy.

You now know what it takes to make a difference, and I encourage you with all my heart to get out there and do it. The rest of the book is devoted to helping you maximize your full potential—and create the life you want.

HIV/AIDS testing, Arusha, Tanzania

Hands for Help School, Arusha, Tanzania

PART II

Eight Principles to Maximize Your True Potential

Gemendhoo Island, the Maldives, after the tsunami

Introduction

Everyone has potential. Unfortunately, not everyone knows how to live up to their potential. There are hundreds of books written to help adults determine and live up to their potential. This is wonderful, and many people benefit from this help, but I thought, what if we didn't wait until we were adults? What if there was something written for kids, by another kid?

Can you imagine what kind of a place the world would be if we used our true potential at an early age? What would we be able to accomplish? I know from my own experience what a child can do, and it is my goal to help as many kids as possible to realize their own true potential.

I want to help you create the life you want, and I want to help you help others. My eight principles can help you reach your full potential. Each principle is followed by a series of exercises, and I encourage you to do all of them. This book started as a trifold flyer with my eight principles listed in it. I designed it to empower children in sub-Saharan Africa, but I soon realized that in order to be more effective, the children needed exercises to understand my principles. Then, when I conducted the workshops, students began asking me more and more questions about the principles and how I had applied them. With all the reviews from these students, I got inspired to reach even more people and started the process of writing everything down. Now I can offer others the same destination of empowerment, but I used different routes like brochures, workbooks, and finally a book, to get there.

After all, life is about participation. No one ever gets anywhere just looking at the road map. You still have to get in the car and drive. Enjoy the journey on your way to reaching your MAXIMUM POTENTIAL!

With Hands for Help members in Mexico

Know Your Destination

What keeps me going is goals.
—MUHAMMAD ALI, "THE GREATEST" BOXER OF ALL TIME

Sometimes that first step of a journey can be hard. Let's go back to the idea of the road map. Whenever you want to travel somewhere, you need to know where you are starting from. That is generally pretty easy. Most people know where they are. The bigger issue is whether you know where you are going. What is your destination?

I bet you have dreams. Take a moment to think about them. It is important for everyone to have dreams. Dreams are full of hope, and hope keeps us going even when life is not easy. But are goals and dreams the same thing? The answer is no. Dreams are those visions of success that pull you forward to meet your goals. Even great dreamers need more imagination to achieve goals than they ever needed to dream in the first place.

You need to set concrete goals in order to achieve your dreams. You also need to believe in your dreams and take responsibility for them. How do you take responsibility for your dreams? By being in charge of completing whatever actions are necessary to make those dreams come true. Here is my personal example of the difference between a dream and a goal and how the goal will help you accomplish your dream.

At my school, St. Andrew's College in Aurora, Ontario, there is an annual reading prize. The student who reads the most books over the school year wins this reading prize. It is based strictly on a reading list appropriate to the grade, so that every student has an equal chance of winning. My dream was to get that prize. What did I need to do to achieve my dream? I knew I needed to read at least twenty-five books. So the reading prize was my dream, and reading twenty-five books was my goal. I broke down the task into small realistic goals (2.5 books per month) and was able to achieve my dream of being awarded this reading prize in June 2007 and again in 2008.

When setting goals, it is wise to have a plan. I talked about the SMART plan in chapter 3 (page 21). This is your road map to success. In addition to the SMART plan, it is also important to write down your goal. Writing it down makes it real. Writing it down also helps bring it into your subconscious mind. Once your subconscious takes hold of it, amazing things will happen.

There are six types of goals that are not so good. These goals imitate real, true, honest goals and it is easy to get fooled by them. These goals come from Kathy Gates, Professional Life Coach.

1. **Sticky Goals:** Goals that you have not been able to achieve and that may not fit into your life anymore. You won't give up on them, because you do not want to let go. You need to look at these goals again, and you need to look at your life. Then you need to either change the goals or let go of them. For example, your goal is a trip with your family to Disney World. You plan it all out and break it down into manageable pieces. You know how much money you need to save. Then your parents tell you that the trip will have to wait for another year, because your grandparents are celebrating their fiftieth wedding anniversary at the exact same time you want to go to Disney World. You plead with them to find a way, and they tell you they can't. However, you continue to tell everyone you are going, because you are still convinced it will happen. You will not let go of the goal or the dream. You would be far better off to adjust your plans and go another time.

2. **Transparent Goals:** Goals that have no plan attached to them. These are often simply actions that do not take you to an end that you desire. For instance, you want to reach the goal of reading twenty-five books during the school year, yet you have no idea how to go about doing it, so you just pick one of the books on the list and start reading. You do not know how much time you should devote to reading, because you have not figured out how many books per week you need to read. It will be much harder this way, because you have not broken a large task down into smaller tasks, and it's much harder to measure how much you have achieved.

3. **Contradictory Goals:** These are goals that are good on their own, but that contradict each other. One goal gets in the way of another goal and you may end up jeopardizing both goals. For example, you have a goal to join the swim team at school; practices and tryouts are every Monday and Thursday after school. You have wanted to be on the team for two years. You also want to be involved in the tutoring program at school. Your goal is to help other students who are having a hard time with their schoolwork. Unfortunately, the tutoring time is Thursday after school. You cannot do both the swim team and the tutoring. You will have to choose which goal is most important to you.

4. **False Goals:** Goals that are for your own glory, to please and gain recognition from others. These goals are not authentic, because they are purely selfish. You are not being true to yourself or others with this kind of goal. For example, you want the lead role in the school play, not because acting is important to you or you feel the role is very special, but because you think it will make you more popular.

5. **Floating Goals:** Goals that never make it out of your head onto paper, let alone become reality. These are goals like "I wish I had some money for a new video game," or "I wish I had that bike." These

goals generally have the words "wish" or "want" attached to them, and they are often quite selfish. Sometimes you can make them into solid goals, but often they are things that you aren't really prepared to take action on.

6. **Blind Goals:** If you write down your goal and plan it out well and then never look at it again, it becomes a blind goal. It will be easy for you to allow your time and energy for these goals to be taken up with the "busyness" of life. For instance, I have always wanted to act in a Harry Potter movie. I have even written down my goal and my plan. I have researched the requirements, but until now have never taken the time to sit down and write letters to the casting agents and directors. I have not been in a movie yet.

To reach a goal, you must take responsibility for your own life. It is easy to pass it off and say that you couldn't do it because you didn't have the time or for some other reason. Truly taking responsibility for your life means that a lot of what happens is up to you. Think of yourself as the architect of your own life. You design the plans, draw up the blueprint and oversee construction. Your parents, family, and teachers help "build" you, because obviously their influence shapes the person you will become. In the final analysis though, it is your plan and your dream.

Feeling in charge of your life is a terrific feeling. When you are ready and willing to take responsibility for creating success and living your dreams, you are in a perfect place to set goals and create plans of action to achieve them. Take charge and set goals.

Knowing your end point can help you develop your personal road map. The destination is more important than the starting point. You may encounter detours and roadblocks along the way, but knowing your destination and following the map will help you achieve your goals. When you know where you are going, then you can break the journey down into manageable pieces. What happens when you don't have a destination firmly set in your mind? You have no way to chart your course. If we use the example of the road trip again, you can pack your car, climb in and pull out of your driveway. You can even think, "I want to go somewhere to the west," and head in that general direction, but you will be driving aimlessly, turning this way and that, unless you have a specific destination in mind. Even if you have a map in the car with you, it will do you no good unless you can draw a path from where you are starting to where you want to go.

How do you figure out your destination? You need to know what is important to you and what you are good at. You also need to know that you are capable of arriving at your destination. By looking closely at your life, your achievements, your capabilities and your talents, you will be able to think about your goals and this will help you create a personal mission statement.

If you have ever heard of a mission statement, you might associate it with a business or organization. However, a personal mission statement is a brief description of what you want to focus on, what you want to accomplish and what kind of person you want to become over the next one to three years. It is a way to focus your energy, actions, behavior and decisions on the things that are most important to you. The following exercises will help you put together your own mission statement. For the purpose of these exercises I will ask you to focus on the year ahead, but you are encouraged to think beyond.

When you have your personal mission statement, then you will be able to draw your road map and you will see your journey clearly in front of you. Here are two more tips to help you plan your goals and make them happen.

1. Your goal must be very personal and mean a lot to you.
2. WRITE YOUR GOALS DOWN! It has been shown time and again that the most successful people write their goals down. Do it in a journal or on your bathroom mirror, but do it. Write it in a positive light. Write it out in complete detail so that when you picture it in your conscious mind, your subconscious mind sees it as well.

When you write down your goals and make them big, you will attain much. And when you write down your goals in detail, with a specific plan of action, you will have a better chance of seeing the road blocks before you stumble on them. Even if you stumble, you can pick yourself up and determine which way to steer if you have a direction to follow. The following exercises will help you create your personal mission statement. Remember that we will focus only on the year ahead for this exercise, but I want you to think beyond. You can also download all these exercises from my website, www.bilaalrajan.com. There is also a link on the Orca website, www.orcabook.com.

Public speaking at a school

Make It Personal

What are your goals for:

1. Spiritual growth
Where do you find peace of mind and meaning in your life?

- **Main Goal:**

- **Must be completed by:**

- **Tasks to do to complete this goal:**

- **Possible challenges:**

2. Personal relationships
How can you improve relationships with your parents, friends, teachers?

- **Main Goal:**

- **Must be completed by:**

- **Tasks to do to complete this goal:**

- **Possible challenges:**

3. Learning
What new skills do you want to acquire?

- **Main Goal:**

- **Must be completed by:**

- **Tasks to do to complete this goal:**

- **Possible challenges:**

4. Social contribution/community service
Which organizations and associations do you want to belong to?
What do you want to do in your community?

- **Main Goal:**
- **Must be completed by:**
- **Tasks to do to complete this goal:**

- **Possible challenges:**

5. Leisure/hobbies
What recreational activities would you like to make time for?

- **Main Goal:**
- **Must be completed by:**
- **Tasks to do to complete this goal:**

- **Possible challenges:**

6. Fitness/health/well-being
What are your goals for your fitness and overall health?

- **Main Goal:**
- **Must be completed by:**
- **Tasks to do to complete this goal:**

- **Possible challenges:**

Notes:

7. Academics
What are your goals for your grades? What are your strongest subjects?

- **Main Goal:**

- **Must be completed by:**

- **Tasks to do to complete this goal:**

- **Possible challenges:**

8. Financial
How are you going to have enough money to do the things you want to do?

- **Main Goal:**

- **Must be completed by:**

- **Tasks to do to complete this goal:**

- **Possible challenges:**

Notes:

My Monthly Goals

Now we are going to start breaking things down.
For each of your goals you will write out a monthly to-do list.
Once you have your monthly goals worked out,
you can break those down further into weekly goals.

Month	To-do	Complete by:
January		
February		
March		
April		
May		
June		
July		
August		
September		
October		
November		
December		

My Weekly Goals

Week	Goal
1	
2	
3	
4	
5	
6	
7	
8	
9	
10	
11	
12	
13	
14	
15	
16	

Making Change

Week	Goal
17	
18	
19	
20	
21	
22	
23	
24	
25	
26	
27	
28	
29	
30	
31	
32	
33	
34	

Principle One: Know Your Destination

Week	Goal
35	
36	
37	
38	
39	
40	
41	
42	
43	
44	
45	
46	
47	
48	
49	
50	
51	
52	

List your Strengths

I am good at:	
I am confident when:	
Some of my proudest achievements are:	
I am proud of them because:	
Which skills would you like to improve upon and develop during the next year?	
When you are not feeling confident or capable, what things might help you turn a negative into a positive?	

Meeting Challenges

Think of a situation where you had an important task to do, and you weren't quite sure how you would be able to accomplish it, but in the end you did!

What was the task?	
What were some of your biggest challenges?	
What were the steps you took to tackle those challenges? How did you make yourself UNcomfortable to challenge yourself?	
What was the outcome and how did you feel about it?	

Making Change

Look again at the list of things you want to accomplish this year, and think about some of the challenges you have identified.

	Goal	Possible challenge
e.g.	Make ten new friends this school year.	I am very shy, so it is hard for me to approach people.
1		
2		
3		
4		
5		
6		

88

Now look at the list of things that you are good at and make you proud. Which of these things will enable you to accomplish some of the goals you have set?	
What skills and knowledge can you use to overcome some of the possible challenges?	
What skills and knowledge will you need to develop further?	
Sometimes to accomplish a goal you just need to push yourself and act with courage. What acts of courage may be necessary to achieve your goals?	

Putting It All Together

Now it's time to use all this information to create your personal mission statement. While there is no unique formula for creating your personal mission statement, the following guidelines may be helpful:

- Keep it simple, clear and brief (three to five sentences long).
- Write about what you want to focus on and who you want to become as a person. Think about specific actions, behaviors, habits and qualities that would have a significant positive impact on you over the next one to three years.
- Make sure your mission statement is positive. Focus on what you want to do or become and use phrases that reinforce the probability of success. For example, say, "I will eat and drink only healthy, nutritious and energizing food and snacks at all meals to complement my daily exercise program of walking one kilometer a day," instead of saying, "I will not eat junk food. I will not watch TV. I will not be a couch potato."
- Include behaviors, character traits and values that you consider particularly important and want to develop further. Your mission statement will guide you in your day-to-day actions and decisions by becoming a part of your everyday life.
- Make it emotional by using adverbs and adjectives. This will make it even more compelling, inspiring and energizing. For example, there is a big difference between saying, "I will learn to play tennis this year," and "I will diligently teach myself in twelve short months how to play outstanding tennis so that I will be nicknamed Roger Federer Junior."
- When you have finished writing your mission statement, put it somewhere you can see it often—a bulletin board, your school locker. Your journey has begun!

Remember that your mission statement is not cast in stone. It will continue to change and evolve as you find out more about yourself and what you want out of each part of your life.

Personal Mission Statement Example

I will improve my grades by five percent this year. I will achieve this by committing to my academic responsibilities. I will focus my organizational skills on reviewing all schoolwork on the day I learn it. I pledge to complete my assignments two days before they are due. To expand my learning and perspective, I will read one book a week from the school's suggested reading list as well as at least one section of the newspaper per week. I will also join one school committee and participate in two community support activities in order to meet new friends and give back to those who need help.

Your personal mission statement helps define how you live your life. Your idea of success and happiness is going to be different from another person's idea of success and happiness. When you create your personal mission statement, you are saying that you recognize your individuality, and you are willing to define what success is to you. Your concept of success and happiness may change over time, but so can your personal mission statement. You just have to get started, and it is my hope that this book and the exercises within it have put you on the right path.

With a reporter in Arusha, Tanzania

Think Before You Act

If you take responsibility for yourself you will develop
a hunger to accomplish your dreams.
—LES BROWN, PUBLIC SPEAKER, AUTHOR AND TELEVISION PERSONALITY

Can you remember when you were really little and you grabbed a toy from someone—your brother or sister or a friend? At that time in your life, you were still learning self-control. A big part of self-control is learning to think before you act. It is about controlling your impulses. Can you do that today?

Thinking before we act is about responding to a situation rather than just reacting to it. Reactions based on emotions can potentially make a situation worse. Responding responsibly means thinking first. It happens when you are able to step back from a situation, assess it and come up with a solution that works for everyone involved. Responding thoughtfully to a situation means being proactive, rather than reactive. As the saying goes: "In case of a medical emergency, check YOUR OWN pulse FIRST!" It gives you a chance to put your feelings into perspective and decide what the best way to handle them or express them might be. You can choose your words and actions carefully, and work to find a kind and gentle solution. You can minimize hurt feelings and you can even ensure that the people involved, including yourself, come out of the situation feeling valued and understood. If you find that your actions are being driven by your emotions, then you need to put them in the freezer to chill for a bit before responding.

Thinking before you act can have a huge impact on your relationships with other people. From the day we are born we interact with others, and we want our interactions to be positive for both parties. After all, we are very social creatures. As human beings, we are responsible for our own attitudes and actions, and we need to recognize and take that responsibility seriously. People of all ages, but especially kids like you and me, often do not take responsibility for their own actions, and when this happens, no one wins.

Take a moment to think about your actions and how they might impact others. Is thinking this way new for you, or do you generally tend to think of others? If you don't, then try to imagine how it might feel to think about someone else. Think about how your actions make other people feel. Think about how you would feel if you were on the receiving end of those actions. In other words, it is good to be able to put yourself in someone else's shoes.

Do you argue with people a lot? Why is that? After all, everyone gets into arguments sometimes. But think of yourself and think of the people you tend to argue with the most. What brings an argument on? Some people feel like they need to be right all the time and must argue a point until they prove themselves, or the other person gets frustrated and gives up. Other people just do not want to open themselves to new ideas. Others are in need of attention. If you tend to argue frequently, think about what causes you to argue.

When an argument or a disagreement is about to happen, you need to think about how you can deal with the potential conflict in a reasonable way. This way you will be able to step back and look at the situation before you say or do something you may regret later. For example, there was a guy named Bill (not his real name) in my class who thought he was the best at every sport. One day in gym, when we were playing floor hockey, Bob (another changed name) successfully ducked past Bill and accidentally bumped into him. Bill became furious, because he thought Bob bumped into him on purpose. He was angry, and he reacted by slashing Bob with his stick and injuring him quite badly. Bob had simply wanted to score a goal. If Bill had waited until after the game to ask Bob why he had bumped into him and listened to the answer, it would have saved a lot of trouble, hurt egos and pain.

I use an approach I call PLOT, which allows you to assess any situation from a safe distance. The letters stand for Prepare, Listen, Observe and be Tactful. I came up with this after many discussions with my family, my friends and my mentors.

P—PREPARE

Remember that words are like arrows, you cannot do anything once you release them into the open air. You need to think about what you need to say and really understand why it is important to you and why it is important that the other person know about it too. If you say what you need to say, will it truly make a difference in the other person's life, or are you trying to make yourself feel important and correct?

L—LISTEN

Remember why God has given you two ears and only one mouth. You need to really use your ears to listen to what another person is trying to say and why. If you do not use your active listening skills, then you are not showing respect for the other person's point of view. When you do not REALLY listen to someone, you are effectively saying that what they think and have to say is not important, or at least not as important as what you have to say. This is no way to avoid an argument. I get into more detail about active listening in Principle Three, page 99.

O—OBSERVE

Be mindful of your posture and the tone and words you choose. Body language is over ninety percent of any message. You may think you are discussing things rationally, but you find that the other person is being defensive. While your words may seem innocent enough, you may not be taking your body language into consideration. You may not be aware, for example, how your sharp tone of voice, your stiff posture or your exaggerated hand gestures affect the other person. Watch carefully the next time you see someone arguing, and you may be surprised that their physical signals often do not match their words.

T—BE TACTFUL

You have to be reasonable and tactful when you are looking for that middle ground—a good compromise. Part of working with someone is understanding that we are all different and we all have different wants and needs. We also have different opinions, and we need to take others' opinions into consideration.

Sometimes it is right for one person to have things their way. Maybe it is an issue that is far more important to that person than it is to you, or maybe they have a special need that you don't have. In these instances, you may have to look closely at how much something really matters to you. If it doesn't matter too much, then give in; when people find you are fair and willing to compromise, they are not as defensive, and arguments occur less frequently as a result. They also will tend to be more flexible on issues unimportant to them.

Handling Conflict Creatively

Think of a time when you had a heated argument/disagreement with someone and things didn't go your way.

Who was it with?	
What was it about?	
Once it was over, how did you feel?	
Think of a time where the outcome was different (things were in your favor). How did you feel?	
Who "won"?	

Making Change

When you think about arguing, which is better?
- ☐ To win and feel empowered? OR
- ☐ To be sure the other person understands your perspective?

Why?	
Who do you argue with most often?	
Why do you think that is?	
What are some other things you can do to resolve a difference of opinion?	
If you had done some things differently during your argument, what would they be?	
Do you think you would have felt differently?	
How do you think the other person would have felt?	

Listen Hard, Don't Hardly Listen

Most of the successful people I've known
are the ones who do more listening than talking.
—**BERNARD BARUCH, FINANCIER AND PRESIDENTIAL POLITICAL ADVISOR**

Communication takes two, and it takes time. As you know, communication is not only about talking. Much of communication takes place through listening. The message you send is not only what you say, it is also how you say it and how you listen to what is being said. To effectively interact with someone, you need to understand them first. Take the time to listen and really hear what they have to say, then communicate with them in a way they will understand.

Of equal importance is paying attention to how your conversation partner communicates. As I mentioned in Part I (pages 40–41), each of us takes in information in a particular way, with a dominant sense. Some "hear" more, others "see" more, and still others "feel" more. Listen to what people say for clues. The following phrases are good examples of how people's choice of words reflects their communication style:

- I can see it all now (seeing)
- In my mind's eye (seeing)
- A gut feeling (feeling)
- I hear you (hearing)
- I had a feeling you were going to say that (feeling)
- That resonates with me (hearing and feeling)

Speech is not the only thing that is important in communication. When we are conversing with someone, we want to establish a rapport or a good relationship with the person right away. As I have mentioned before, body language is an important part of communication and constitutes the majority of what we are communicating. You need to be aware of your own and the other person's speech, mannerisms, body movements and gestures. Once you can see how someone communicates, you must learn to mirror them. Don't worry, they won't notice a thing. For example, you are sitting down and having a conversation with a person. When they cross their legs, five seconds later you should do the same thing. If they wave their hands or nod their head, you should do the same. Their subconscious mind is what notices the mirroring, and it is flattered by the attention. That leaves the conscious mind free to enjoy the conversation. Why is this so important? When you are talking to someone, you are most likely conveying information to that person. You want to be sure that he or she understands everything you are saying.

Active listening is crucial, because when you are listening actively, your conversation partner feels important and valued. Nothing is worse than talking to someone who is looking past you, doing other things or just plain fidgeting. You must learn to look people in the eye and concentrate on what they are saying.

Imagine a person who is going to an interview for a job at a local restaurant. As he is being questioned by the manager, he is looking around the restaurant, not at her. His hands are fidgeting, and he is playing with the zipper on his backpack. He rarely looks her in the eye, and even though he answers all of her questions appropriately, do you think he left a good impression? Right after this interview, the manager has scheduled another one. This person walks in, gives a firm handshake and sits down. All the time the manager is talking to him he is looking her in the eye, unless she is pointing something out to him on paper or in the restaurant. This person is very attentive. Who do you think she is going to hire?

Pay attention to how you interact with your family, because they are the people you converse with most often, and they are also the people you are most likely to be inattentive with. However, they deserve your full attention. Whether you are just joking around, chatting over the dinner table or having a formal family meeting, you must show them the respect of listening and communicating well. You will be surprised at what a difference it will make. And you will get lots of opportunity to practice your active listening skills.

Participating in an HIV/AIDS lifeskills class in Malawi

Understanding Body Language

Using pictures from books, magazines, catalogs, the Internet or even your own personal photos, find pictures of people whose body language represents the following emotions. Once you have picked a picture, look at it carefully to figure out what body language is associated with each emotion.

Emotion	Details
Happy/Excited	
Thoughtful	
Proud	
Distracted	
Angry	
Curious	
Bored	
Hurried	
Sad/Upset	
Attentive	

IOU—Importance Over Urgency

The key is not to prioritize what's on your schedule,
but to schedule your priorities.

—STEPHEN COVEY, COFOUNDER OF FRANKLINCOVEY
AND BEST-SELLING MOTIVATIONAL AUTHOR

Life is busy, and there are lots of things to be done…yesterday! One way to sort through the chaos is to prioritize, which means to decide what is important and what is not. Prioritizing is one of the greatest skills you will ever learn. No matter where you use it—in school, in your career when you grow up, in your chores or in your extracurricular activities—knowing how to prioritize is an essential tool.

Prioritizing reduces stress. Setting a goal and understanding the relative importance of each task in achieving that goal will reduce obstacles to success. Plan ahead, and urgent things will take care of themselves. In other words, when you prioritize you are able to see what tasks are more important than others. You are then able to concentrate on these tasks instead of less important tasks. For example, Fred and Richard are talking about a history exam they are about to take. Fred is extremely tired, because he has stayed up the whole night studying. He is not very happy. Richard is quite calm, because he has had a good night's sleep. He has been studying every day for over a week. Richard asks Fred when he found out about the exam, and Fred tells him that he has known about it for two weeks. Two weeks ago, the exam was important. Richard prioritized and learned the material. By not studying, the exam became urgent for Fred. So make sure to take care of the important issues before they become urgent. This will save you a lot of frustration and time, and everyone will be happier.

In my own life, I find that as I travel quite a bit all over the world, I need to prepare for my assignments, projects and tests weeks ahead of the final due date so that I don't fall behind. It helps me to keep on top of the workload.

Being able to prioritize can sometimes be challenging and is often influenced by how much you enjoy an activity instead of how important it is. This results in a list that is overwhelming and impossible to accomplish. Establishing the relative importance of each item on your list can help you plan out the best order in which to accomplish things. The importance must be determined by what is happening in your own life and by your own goals, responsibilities and dreams. When you make your list, think of the desired end results. Make sure your priorities take these results into consideration. Anything else can be taken off your list.

Do you have to be the one who does everything on your list? Are there other people who can take on some of the responsibility for items on the list? Asking for help from someone else who is willing and capable can be a significant way to reduce the number of items on your list. By delegating, your life will become more manageable. Many people try to do it all, because they think their way is the best or only way, or that nothing will get done properly unless they do it themselves. These are the people who burn out. These are the people who are always stressed and rarely take time for themselves. Learn to delegate where appropriate. It will save you much time, energy and sanity as well. For example, I delegated most of my organization's website setup to other more capable people, even though I had a good understanding of how to do it myself.

Now, about the lists themselves. How many items do you have on your daily to-do list? If you have twenty items, do you REALLY think you are going to get everything done in one day? Are you placing unrealistic expectations on yourself? What about ten items? This is more manageable, but possibly still unrealistic. It is recommended that you have no more than six items on your list on any given day. Any more is overwhelming.

It has been proven that the most productive and successful people make lists. It has also been proven that when you cross something off a list, it has a very positive psychological impact on you. What happens when you have too many things on your list, when they do not all get crossed off? It creates a feeling of failure, which is not good for your self-confidence or your self-esteem. Make sure that you are not your own worst enemy.

Painting batiks in Thailand

Prioritizing Your Life

What are your responsibilities—the things you do every day as part of your commitment to your family, or things that other people are depending on you for? Make a list of the things you are responsible/accountable for.
(E.g., doing my best at school, keeping my bedroom clean and tidy, looking after my little sister after school etc.) Include things that are related to the goals expressed in your personal mission statement.

Daily Commitments

Now, make a list of all the things you want to do in the next week.
Try and make the list as complete as possible, including homework assignments,
sports and other things you have committed to, as well as the day-to-day things
like cleaning your room. Don't forget the fun stuff too. Include the time frame for
the item—when you plan on doing it, or when it needs to be completed by.

Weekly Goals and Responsibilities

Things to Do	Time Frame	Importance	Priority

Now think about why each item is on your list.
Is it a responsibility, or part of a bigger goal? Think about how it fits
into a bigger picture and put a 1, 2 or 3 in the Importance column
(1 = most important; 3 = least important)
Finally, considering both the time frame and the importance,
number the items in order of priority. (1 = highest priority; 3 = lowest priority)
To ensure that you can complete all your high-priority items, are there any changes
you can make (e.g., change the timing, delegate the task)?

Possible changes to list

Possible removal from list

What you will have left is a list of things that you really need to concentrate on. Make a fresh list here with a weekly breakdown of your high-priority items.

My Prioritized Weekly To-Do List

Things to Do	Timing

*With Craig Kielburger, Bilaal's mentor in the Governor-General's
Order of Canada Mentorship Program*

Strength in Numbers

It's easier to be ignorant and say I don't know about the problem.
But once you know, once you've seen it in their eyes, then you
have a responsibility to do something. There is strength in numbers,
and if we all work together as a team, we can be unstoppable.
—CRAIG KIELBURGER, FOUNDER OF FREE THE CHILDREN

Teambuilding

In chapter 4 (page 29), I talked about the advantages of working with a
team. Here are a few exercises to help you build an amazing team.

With the Hands for Help Team at the World Partnership Walk in 2005

Teambuilding

You have to get a package to someone who lives a thousand miles away. To get the package there, it has to travel across a variety of different landscapes. The package is very valuable and must not be destroyed or damaged in any way. For each leg of the journey, each member of your team must choose an animal (not a human) that can safely cross the terrain without too much trouble.

Think creatively about the animals you choose; the best choice may not be the most obvious one. For example, you may think a camel is the best animal to cross the desert, but someone else may choose a cheetah, because it is faster. Remember there is no right answer, just a good choice as expressed by someone other than you.

Terrain	Animal	Why did you choose this animal?
Across a field with very tall grass & bushes		
Through the dark and dangerous jungle/forest		
Across a large body of water		
Across a desert		
Over some mountains		
Following a river		

After all team members have completed the exercise, you will find that there are various different animals that are best suited to each situation. Your opinion may not necessarily be the ideal solution, but by learning what others would do in these situations, you will all benefit by seeing everyone else's unique solutions. In this way, your team can choose the best solution from all those presented.

Who's On Your Team?

When you are working on a group project, it is always fun to work with friends, but sometimes to get the best result you need to work with people whose ideas will challenge the way you think.

In this exercise you are starting a day camp program at Camp Lotsafun, and you are responsible for hiring the staff. Your goal is to hire the best people to create a camp that offers a safe and fun experience.

Think about all the people you know: friends, family, teachers, coaches, etc. For each role, identify someone you feel is best suited for the job. Avoid choosing people just because you like them. Think more about their personalities, their skills, strengths and weaknesses, and how well suited they are for the role. Include yourself.

HINTS:

- Avoid choosing people who all have the same type of personality. Instead select people who will complement each other in their roles.
- Focus on the skills and personalities, not on age or current abilities. (E.g., Grandma might be your fitness coordinator, because she used to be an Olympic athlete; your little sister might be the arts and crafts teacher, because she is so artistic.)
- To start, you can put more than one name in each box, or you can put the same name in more than one box.
- Once you've considered all the roles and possible people, put a star beside the person you want to hire.
- A person can be hired for a maximum of two roles.

Teambuilding

Role (# of positions)	Required Skills	Best Candidates
Camp Director (1)	• Well organized • Deals well with pressure • Strong leader • Good at resolving issues and conflicts	
Treasurer (1)	• Well organized, responsible • Thrifty	
Cook (1)	• Adventurous appetite—willing to try new foods from different cultures • Makes good choices in their personal diet	
Counselors (3)	• Responsible • Fun to be around • Good leaders • Patient	
Lifeguards (2)	• Healthy and fit • Good swimmer • Knows First Aid • Works well under pressure	
Camp Medical/Safety Staff (1)	• Likes taking care of people	

Role (# of positions)	Required Skills	Best Candidates
Special Activities Coordinator (1)	• Has creative ideas • Is good at engaging others in an activity • Good planner • Lots of enthusiasm	
Arts & Crafts Teacher (1)	• Artistic/creative	
Fitness Coordinator (1)	• Healthy & physically active • Encouraging • Makes healthy choices	
Outdoor Education Coordinator (1)	• Knowledgeable about nature and geography • Likes a little adventure	
Homesick Monitor (1)	• Sensitive to people's feelings • Likes taking care of people • Can easily cheer people up	
Maintenance Staff (2)	• Good at repairing things • Good at solving problems • Patient	

Notes:

Getting to Know Your Team

**Choose for your team two people you know but don't normally hang out with.
Consider what you know about each of them,
and for each person write down three characteristics.**

1. Name:

   Characteristics:

2. Name:

   Characteristics:

For Person #1, think of a situation or problem where your personality might complement theirs. What was the situation and how could you help each other?

Think of a situation or problem where Person #2 might have been able to help you solve the problem. What was the situation and how could they help?

*With students in Atlantic Canada to kick off a
fundraising campaign for schools in Africa*

At an HIV training session in Tengeru, Tanzania

The gift of a soccer ball in Malawi

Practice a No-Lose Policy

Adopt a new philosophy of cooperation in which everybody wins.
—W. EDWARDS DEMING, FATHER OF THE QUALITY REVOLUTION

We all want to win. I don't mean that life is a race, although sometimes it can seem that way. What I mean is that everyone wants things to turn out to their advantage as much as possible. While this is not always possible, it is possible to do your best to ensure that everyone has a chance at winning. Turn all situations into win–win! When a situation is win–win, everyone walks away feeling valued and positive—they come away with more than they had before. Stephen Covey's book, *The 7 Habits of Highly Successful People*, goes into these ideas in great detail. The four situations that are most likely to occur as you work to achieve your goals are:

- **Lose–lose:** This happens when, for example, you lose to another person in soccer. Instead of congratulating the winner, you insult them or call them a name, so everyone ends up feeling bad.
- **Lose–win:** This happens when you are feeling sorry for yourself because you didn't win, or you lose just to help the other person win. This is not good, because you are purposely destroying your confidence and self-esteem.
- **Win–lose:** This happens when you are boastful in order to put down another person.

- **Win–win:** This happens when you find a middle ground where everyone can gain something out of the situation. For example, a student who is good at sports but not at schoolwork can help a person who is not good at sports but is a great student, and vice versa. Everyone wins.

Look for ways you can benefit, even when you fall short of a goal or when you find a situation has not worked out to your advantage. For example:

- What did you learn from the situation?
- What would you do differently next time?
- How much of your goal did you achieve?
- Most importantly, look inside yourself to define your own success by canceling competitive comparisons.

When we compare ourselves to others, we certainly do not win, nor does anyone else. Every person is an individual, and when we try to compare ourselves with others, we are comparing apples to oranges. Each of us has unique gifts. You are unique and special, so what is there to gain by comparing yourself to someone else when there is no one else like you? Think how boring the world would be if we were all the same. Comparing does not bring about a Win/Win situation. Someone always loses.

Finding the Upside

Think of a recent situation where you fell short of a goal. Describe the situation. What was the goal? In what way did you fail to reach it?

Identify three things you did well/right.

If there were other people involved, identify three things they did well/right.

If you could change three things about how you prepared, what would they be?

When there is an official competition like a soccer game, obviously not everybody can win, but you can still come away a winner, even if your team loses. Every time we put ourselves out there, stick our necks out, take a risk, we win by summoning the courage to participate. Next time we might be able to do more, and we might succeed. Take the time to acknowledge the little victories, and the bigger ones will come. To learn from our experiences we need to take the time to reflect upon them. One way is to keep a daily journal. You can ask yourself questions that highlight your achievements.

I was inspired to do this by Anthony Robbins' book *Giant Steps*. The reflection questions I ask myself daily are:

- What did I enjoy the most today?
- What am I most excited or happy about today?
- What did I learn today?
- What did I do that made me proud today?
- What commitment am I making today to improve my life?
- What acts of kindness have I done today?
- What did I do today to get me closer to my goals?
- What am I grateful for today?
- What didn't I achieve today that I need to follow up on tomorrow?

Think of other questions that are specific to your goals, and reflect on them daily.

The Joy of Journaling

Journaling is a very powerful tool. There are many reasons to keep a journal, and there are many types of journals. You can keep a daily journal that is about your whole life, and you can also devote a journal specifically to your dreams and goals. Either way, a journal allows you to:

- Chart your progress
- Express your feelings
- Work out tough situations
- Solve problems
- Celebrate victories

Many people are concerned that they cannot write well, but with journals that really doesn't matter. Your journal is personal and, unless you choose to share it with someone, it should be for your eyes only. As long as the writing *feels* good to you, it *is* good for you. You can write anything you like: prose, poetry, stories or songs. And you are not limited to words either. You can use artwork as well. Any means to get your thoughts and feelings out are great ways to journal. You can doodle your way to happiness and contentment in your journal.

Keeping notes in Malawi

My Daily Journal

Name		Date		Day	

What did I enjoy the most today?

1
2
3
4
5

Today I am excited or most happy about:

1
2
3
4
5

Today I learned about:

1
2
3
4
5

What am I most proud of today?

1
2
3
4
5

What commitment am I making to improve my life?

1
2
3
4
5

Who do I love, who loves me?

1
2
3
4
5

Principle Six: Practice a No-Lose Policy

	What did I do today to get to my priority goals?		**What acts of kindness have I done today?**
1		1	
2		2	
3		3	
4		4	
5		5	

	What acts of courage am I going to take tomorrow to improve my life?		**Today I am grateful for:**
1		1	
2		2	
3		3	
4		4	
5		5	

Notes:

Surf's up in Hawaii

Give Yourself a Tune-Up

There's never enough time to do all the nothing you want.
—BILL WATTERSON, AUTHOR OF THE CARTOON STRIP *CALVIN AND HOBBES*

Like a car, your body knows when it is out of balance, and it lets you know. The question is, do you know how to listen to it? There are all kinds of ways in which your body lets you know when something is wrong, or when you need to slow down and take a break. You need to know the signs. So many people do not take a break or get extra sleep when they feel tired. They simply continue to push themselves. Many people do not stop to eat when they are hungry. However, there are even more signs that something is wrong or that you need a break.

Sometimes the body gets sick when we are run-down. Do you stop and rest when you are sick, or do you keep going? Maybe you have stiff muscles and joints. Maybe you experience headaches, stomachaches, or feel really stressed out or tired, anxious or depressed. The list could go on and on, but do you know what to do about it?

Make sure you take time to give yourself a tune-up—to rejuvenate yourself physically, mentally, spiritually and socially. You are made up of more than just your physical body. Your mind also needs rest and rejuvenation, and so does your soul. You need to find the time to rest, relax and, most importantly, to laugh. Find that place that gives you energy, and take the time to go there and visit "with yourself." Discover ways to be a human *being*, not just a human *doing*.

When I am traveling a lot, doing a lot of public speaking and feeling tired, I like to take a plunge in a cold pool to relax. This helps me tremendously to unwind and revitalize my body and mind. It may not be your idea of relaxation, but it works for me. Figure out what rejuvenates you, and commit to taking the time to do it.

Taking good care of yourself is more than just eating right and getting exercise; it involves taking time to think and feel. Sometimes it can be difficult to fit it into your schedule, but you can often discover opportunities to find that "place" just through the activities you choose or people you spend time with.

Four Ways to Find Your Bliss

1. PHYSICALLY

We get tired, thirsty and hungry, and when we do, our bodies let us know. Without food, water and sleep, we would die. To care for yourself physically, you must:

- Get plenty of rest. Make sure you are not staying up half the night working, playing video games or studying. If you are prioritizing well and not overloading yourself, then you will not need to work into the night.
- Eat a well-balanced diet low in sugar and processed foods and high in whole foods and raw foods. Stay away from fast food if you can. I need to work on this too, so don't think you are alone.
- Get lots of exercise and fresh air. Walk more, ride your bike, find physical activities that you like to do, because if you don't like them you won't do them and that would defeat the purpose. If you don't know what you like, explore your options. You might find you enjoy yoga, rock climbing, hiking, swimming, soccer or any number of other activities.

2. MENTALLY

Chances are your mind gets lots of exercise in school. This may be all you need, or you may find that you need more intellectual stimulation. You also have the holidays and summer vacation to think about. Keeping your mind sharp during these periods is important. You want your imagination to be stimulated by what you do. Again, you must find things that are interesting to you. I write my books during the holidays, and I don't take any schoolwork home. I work hard enough during the school year. If you try to read the newspaper because your parents do, but you do not enjoy it, you will not get all you can from the experience. Here are a few suggestions to help you exercise yourself mentally:

- Read whatever truly interests you. It doesn't matter if it is fact or fiction, magazines or books. As long as it interests you, your mind will soak it up, and your imagination will soar. TV does not stimulate your imagination, so try not to watch it all the time!
- Try doing crossword puzzles, word puzzles, Sudoku, Brainquest, Mathquest or other math puzzles. Or play board games like Monopoly or Risk. Some other games that I love playing are Blokus, Cranium and Geo Bee.
- Paint, write, draw, sculpt or do any other creative activity. These will keep your mind active and happy.
- Have deep discussions with someone. Debate and learn about new things.
- Take field trips, whether they are in your backyard, on a camping trip or to another country. Learn about where you are going and observe while you are there.
- Keep a journal. (See Principle Six, page 122.)
- Visit a museum or art gallery.

3. SPIRITUALLY

This is a very important aspect of your well-being. It doesn't matter what you or your family believe in as long as you have FAITH in something. There are so many people who do not have faith in anything, and without faith, it is pretty hard to have hope. There are many different spiritual paths and religions, and they all have something to offer. Belief in God or some sort of higher power can be extremely beneficial and comforting. Having a spiritual connection with nature and the cycle of life is important too. Here are a few ideas to help you connect spiritually:

Meditation: This is one of the most beneficial things you can do for your body, mind and spirit, and it could easily have fit into any of the other categories. Meditation helps the mind focus, helps relax the body and helps us connect spiritually. Meditation can do amazing things in your life. In schools that have fifteen minutes of meditation first thing in the morning, the students' grades went up and their stress levels decreased substantially. Why is this? The benefits of meditation are tremendous and plentiful, and doctors all over the world are realizing how effective it can be when it comes to helping their patients. The following list includes just some of the benefits of meditation:

- Relaxation
- Reduction of stress, anxiety and depression
- Increased focus and concentration
- Enhanced spiritual connections
- Improved breathing
- Increased level of creativity
- Increased learning ability and better memory
- Increased ability to visualize
- Self-confidence

I encourage you to read more about meditation and find a style that works for you.

Prayer: I don't know how many people pray, but I know it works. Pray to your higher power or just send a message out to the universe. Either way, you will find it works. I don't mean pray to get more money or better grades or a new bike. I mean pray for guidance and peace in life or in a specific situation. You will be surprised how much it will help.

Congregation: For many people, attending a church, mosque, temple or some sort of spiritual gathering is extremely nourishing to the soul.

Nature: Get outside as often as you can. Being out in nature helps us to connect with ourselves in a way nothing else can. Just feeling the sunlight on your skin and breathing in the fresh air is rejuvenating. Watch the sunset and listen to how your soul feels.

Breathing: Good breathing techniques are very useful for eliminating stress, helping the body physically and making you feel more spiritually connected. There are a lot of good books and websites about breathing exercises and techniques.

4. SOCIALLY

Having a sense of community is crucial to well-being! Humans are very social creatures, and most of us need to have contact with others. We need to feel a sense of belonging. There are many different types of communities: your family, neighborhood, sports team, school, spiritual or religious community. Think about what communities you are a part of. Here are some suggestions for how to become more socially connected:

- Have a heart-to-heart talk with someone in your family.
- Make a special effort to hang out with your friends on a regular basis.

- Contribute to your community. Help clean up your neighborhood, participate in a bake sale or take a leadership role.
- Share a personal story with someone you trust.
- Go to the movies with family or friends. Talk about the movie afterward.

Rejuvenation

Some activities completely change your mood and provide you with mental, spiritual and physical energy. Incorporating more or less of a certain activity may help give you the boost you need.

Think about all the different things you do, then think about how they make you feel. Provide examples of activities that bring out certain moods.

Ski racing on Blue Mountain (PHOTO IAN DUNIN)

What Activities Make You Feel...

Intelligent	
Energized	
Bored	
Connected to the world	
Calm	
Gross	
Brave	
Silly	
Creative	
Joyful	

Making Change

How Do You Feel When You...

Walk through the woods	
Volunteer	
Talk to your parents about an important event	
Watch TV even when none of your favorite shows are on	
Sit by a stream/lake/river	
Go to church/temple/ place of worship	
Finish your homework ahead of schedule	
Read/write a letter or story	

Principle Seven: Give Yourself a Tune-Up

Play a sport/exercise	
Argue with your sister/brother/friend	
Watch a sport where you know some of the players	
Do something kind without being asked to	
Accomplish something you never did before	
Spend time with your parent/grandparent one on one	
Visit a museum/place of interest	
Listen to music	

Sometimes people can impact our moods just by being themselves.
Think about the people in your life and identify people who make you feel...

Confident	
Energized	
Safe	
Frustrated	
Intimidated	
Angry	

Your perfect day
If you could spend one day doing anything, what would you do?

Who would you choose to do it with and why?

Did you know it takes only thirty days to create or break a habit?
Changing habits can provide new energy that can be used in other activities.
Think about some of your habits.

What are your worst habits?	
Pick one habit you would like to change. What are some of the barriers that prevent you from changing?	
What can you do to try and overcome those barriers?	

Commit a month to overcoming those barriers and changing that habit.

What are your best habits?	
What are three habits you observe and admire in other people?	

Pick one good new habit and commit a month to adding it into your life,
OR increase your commitment to one of your existing good habits.

137

Left to right: Justin Ford, Bilaal, Jonathan Tse

Visualize Success

I would visualize things coming to me. It would just make me feel better. Visualization works if you work hard. That's the thing. You can't just visualize and go eat a sandwich.

—JIM CARREY, CANADIAN COMEDIAN AND ONE OF THE HIGHEST-PAID FILM ACTORS IN THE WORLD

D id you know we can trick our brains? It's true. When we imagine something, our brain cannot tell the difference between that and reality. When we imagine something, our brain reacts as though it is truly happening. We experience the feelings that we would feel if it was real, and we can turn this to our advantage, especially when we imagine that we have already accomplished our goals.

Think of it this way. Imagine something that you don't like to do. Maybe you don't like cleaning your room. You dread the task every Saturday morning, and that dread hangs over you as the weekend approaches. However, it is your responsibility, and you have to follow through with it. When we dread something, we are using our imagination. We are imagining doing it and remembering how awful it is and how much we dislike it. Our feelings match this, and we feel frustration at having to do the task, even before we have to do it. It just doesn't seem fair.

Now try this. Instead of imagining doing the task, imagine what your room will look like when you have finished cleaning it. Imagine it already done. Picture in your mind what your room looks like. Picture all your books placed on your shelf. See your clean desk with your schoolwork piled neatly in one corner and all your pens and pencils, rulers and erasers stored in the appropriate place. Imagine that you can see the floor, your chair and the top of your dresser, because all your clothes have been picked up and either put away properly or put in the laundry basket. Visualize your bed neatly made.

How do you feel? Do you feel a sense of accomplishment as you look around this room? Does the tidiness give you a sense of peace and calm? Does it remove stress? Now keep this image in your mind while you actually clean your room, always picturing the completed task. You will be amazed at how quickly it gets done and how pleasant it is to complete. If you keep the positive emotions (my room looks great!) in your mind instead of dwelling on the negative emotions (I hate cleaning my room!), you will feel a world of difference.

Creating Your Vision

Visualizing is about looking inside. See in your mind a place and time where your goal has already been achieved. Then, look for the things in that vision that created the success and prepare a vision board. It doesn't matter if you are visualizing cleaning your room or raising a million dollars. The principle is the same.

Similar to a mission statement, being able to picture or visualize our future can help us find a way to achieve a goal. Create a vision for your life. Decide where you want to go and picture yourself actually achieving success at each critical milestone. Visualization helps us learn to use our dreams to fuel our vision and stay focused on it. People who take opportunities and make something of them are the ones who are successful. They are successful because they have a vision of what they can do and what they can be. This is why visualization is so important. It is a tool for us to use so that we can think about what we WILL have in our lives. When we do that, we will attract it. We have to visualize what we want in our lives as if we already have it. The rest will follow.

Create your vision with careful thought and planning. Your vision can begin with a simple desire, but it can't end there. Develop a clear vision of how to fulfill your desire. When you visualize, you open yourself up to the help of the universe. Listen to your intuition. Feel it, and slow down to be guided by your higher power. Have a vision for your life, decide where you want to go and create your vision step-by-step. Here are some examples.

For the last several years, each person in my family has created a personal vision board, and we also contribute to a family vision board. We use bristol board and images from the Internet and magazines, and sort them into nine categories: academics, financial, fitness and health, contribution to community, learning, business, spirituality, relationships and leisure. We put our vision boards into inexpensive frames and hang them on the wall, where we can look at them all the time.

Here is an example of the power of the vision board. In the summer of 2007, I was supposed to go to Jamaica on a field trip with UNICEF Canada. Due to unavoidable circumstances, the plans changed three days prior to departure. Our new destination was Africa. During the trip we stopped in Egypt on our way to Tanzania, our volunteering destination. After we got back, my aunt pointed out that we had achieved one of our family's vision board goals: to visit the Aga Khan Mausoleum in Aswan, Egypt. We were shocked, because we had forgotten that we had put this goal on our vision board in December 2005! This has happened to me not once, but many times. I put a picture of the volcanoes in Hawaii on my vision board, and I saw them last summer. I also put a picture of my book on it, and now you have my book in your hands.

Open Your Eyes

Every morning on my way to school, I use a special visualization technique that I learnt from coaches and motivational speakers like Tony Robbins and Dave Austin.

1. Look at something in nature and take note of three things about it that you have never noticed before, like droplets of moisture on a leaf or on a spider's web.
2. Close your eyes and visualize all these glorious details.
3. Now think of five things that you are grateful for.
4. Eyes still closed, surround yourself with white light and love.
5. Visualize your immediate family (very close loved ones), and surround them with white light, love and positive energy.
6. Do the same for your best friends and even your foes. For school, I add my fellow students, teachers, schoolwork and activities.
7. Meditate. I meditate quietly on my mantra (any name or phrase that makes you feel good) to feel peace, but you can choose whatever works for you. It could be as simple as a picture of rose or a loved one.
8. In your mind's eye, with eyes closed, picture a set of gates in front of you.
9. See them open and watch yourself enter. What you see next is the most beautiful thing in the world according to you. Feel it as if you are already living it, and watch this beautiful thing become even more amazing by the second.
10. Then you see another pair of gates, exit through them and arrive in the present moment, truly content. Once again, enter the gates and take another look at the marvelous image you created. Now open your eyes.

In grade six, I was having real problems in English. I changed my English grade with this type of visualization. I visualized my report card with an A grade on it. By doing this exercise every day, I was able to bring my English mark up to an A. I also greatly improved my relationship with my teacher, Mrs. Bartlett, at St. Andrew's College. The motivation she gave me inspired me to write even more, and this book is a direct result of that visualization.

Similar to a mission statement, being able to picture or visualize our future can help us find our way along the path to achieving a goal.

Create a vision for your life, decide where you want to go, and picture yourself actually achieving success at each of the critical milestones.

Personal Vision Board

Using pictures from books, magazines, catalogs, the Internet or your own personal photos, make a collage of pictures that represent the things you most want to achieve.

Focusing on the future, use pictures of people accomplishing the things you want to do. Acknowledge the past by including images of events that put you on the path to being the person you are today. The following categories will help you create your vision board. The idea is to ensure that you have a vision for each area of your life:

1. Fitness and health—physical, mental, spiritual and emotional
2. Contribution/charity/community—fundraising and volunteering
3. Fun time—relaxation, vacations and hobbies
4. Financial—income, savings and investments
5. Business—growth, sales and new ventures
6. Relationships—immediate family, friends and business
7. Personal—projects, purchases and hobbies
8. Academics—grades and classes, learning new things
9. Awards—school, church/religious, sports, and other clubs and organizations

A vision board can be short, medium or long-term and should be reviewed frequently. Surround yourself with the images; put them up in your room so you can look at them often. Spend time looking at the pictures and thinking about your own successes. You will be amazed at how visualization can really build up your confidence and help you step up to meet your goals.

Imagine...

Using your imagination, describe your future as you see it.
Picture yourself in a year:

Where are you living?	
What school do you go to?	
What are your classes?	
How are your grades?	
What are your achievements for this year?	
Are you in any leadership roles? (class president, team captain, tutor, mentor)	
What are your personal interests? Sports? Hobbies?	
Do you belong to any Clubs? Groups? Organizations? What do they stand for?	
What kind of charity/ volunteer work do you do?	

144

Principle Eight: Visualize Success

Picture yourself in five years:	
Where are you living?	
What school do you go to?	
What are you studying/ your classes?	
How are your grades?	
Who are your friends? (Same friends as before or different ones?)	
What are your achievements in the past five years?	
What are your personal interests? Sports? Hobbies?	
Do you belong to any Clubs? Groups? Organizations? What do they stand for?	
Are you in any leadership roles?	
What kind of charity/ volunteer work do you do?	

	Now picture yourself in twenty-five years:
Where are you living?	
Do you live alone?	
Are you employed?	
What do you do for a living?	
Who do you work for?	
What college/university did/do you attend?	
If you are still in school, what are you studying?	
What sort of vehicle do you drive? What year, make, color? Do you own it or lease it?	
What are your personal interests? Sports? Hobbies?	
Do you belong to any Clubs? Groups? Organizations? What do they stand for?	
What kind of charity/ volunteer work do you do?	
What do you do on weekends?	
What do you do for spiritual fulfillment? Do you meditate? Do you belong to a church/ place of worship?	

Final Thoughts

Our dreams are those visions of success that pull us forward to meet our goals. Even great dreamers need imagination to achieve goals. They also need to believe in their dreams as well as take responsibility for being in charge of doing whatever is necessary to make those dreams come true.

Being in charge of your life is a terrific feeling. When you are ready and willing to take responsibility for creating success and living your dreams, you are in a perfect position to set goals and implement a plan of action. It all starts with a question…

What Is My Vision for My Life?

The concepts in this book are ones that many people do not have a firm grasp on. It will benefit you greatly to understand these concepts and principles now. Then when you move into adulthood, you will have the toolkit for success.

Now think about your coming year: What can you do this year? This month? This week? What can you do TODAY? The answer…

Take charge. Set goals. Take action!

I would love to hear how you put what you learned from this book into action. You can always contact me through my website at www.bilaalrajan.com. The website gets an amazing number of hits per month, so lots of people must be learning about what can be done to help children in need in different parts of the world. My organization and website are realities that help others, and you can do the same in whatever way you choose. Go for it, and good luck to you all! Remember: Together We Can Make a Difference.

With Hands for Help students in Arusha, Tanzania

The journey of a thousand leagues begins with a single step.
So we must never neglect any work of peace within our reach,
however small.

—ADLAI E. STEVENSON, AMERICAN STATESMAN

AND US AMBASSADOR TO THE UN

With author and activist Eric Walters, 2008

Bilaal's Reading List

Arden, Paul. *It's Not How Good You Are, It's How Good You Want to Be*

Bennett, Bo. *Year to Success*

Buzan, Tony. *Brain Child: How Smart Parents Make Smart Kids*
—*How to Mind Map*

Canfield, Jack (editor). *Chicken Soup for the Kid's Soul (Books 1 and 2)*
—*Chicken Soup for the Teenage Soul (Books 1 and 2)*

Castle, Caroline. *For Every Child: The UN Convention on the Rights of the Child*

Clason, George. *The Richest Man in Babylon*

Covey, Sean. *The 7 Habits of Highly Effective Teens*
—*The 6 Most Important Decisions You'll Ever Make: A Guide for Teens*

Covey, Stephen. *The 7 Habits of Highly Successful People*

Dorling Kindersley. *A Life Like Mine*

Dyer, Wayne W. and Kristina Tracy. *Incredible You! 10 Ways to Let Your Greatness Shine Through*

Edelman, Marian Wright. *I Can Make a Difference: A Treasury to Inspire Our Children*

Eker, T. Harv. *Secrets of the Millionaire Mind: Mastering the Inner Game of Wealth*

Ellis, Deborah. *The Heaven Shop*

Gandhi, Mahatma. *Gandhi: An Autobiography: The Story of My Experiments With Truth*

Hill, Napoleon. *Think and Grow Rich* (book and audio)

Ilibagiza, Immaculée. *Left to Tell: Discovering God Amidst the Rwandan Holocaust*

Jamal, Azim and Harvey McKinnon. *The Power of Giving: Creating Abundance in Your Home, at Work and in Your Community.*

Kielburger, Craig and Marc Kielburger. *Me to We: Finding Meaning in a Material World*

Kiyosaki, Robert T. and Sharon Lechter. *Rich Dad Poor Dad for Teens —Rich Kid Smart Kid*

Mandela, Nelson. *Long Walk to Freedom: The Autobiography of Nelson Mandela*

Millman, Dan. *Way of the Peaceful Warrior: A Book that Changes Lives*

Robbins, Anthony. *Giant Steps*

Shoveller, Herb. *Ryan and Jimmy: And the Well in Africa that Brought Them Together*

Thomas, Marlo and Christopher Cerf. *Thanks & Giving All Year Long*

Two-Can (editors). *Stand Up, Speak Out*

Walters, Eric. Each and every book!

Willis, Mariaemma and Victoria Kindle Hodson. *Discover Your Child's Learning Style*

Stone Soup magazine

Guinness World Records annual

Workshops

I have been fortunate to attend workshops (live, online or on video) by: Anthony Robbins (Unleash the Power Within for Teens); T. Harv Eker (Millionaire Mind Intensive; Passive Income); Dr. Wayne Dyer (Power of Intention); Mark Victor Hansen; Deepak Chopra; Youth in Motion (Courage to Soar); Craig and Marc Kielburger (Me to We); Martin Wales, Alex Mandossian and Loral Langemeier (Living Out Loud). These were amazing experiences; I highly recommend workshops as a way to soak up new ideas, find motivation and be inspired.

With Deepak Chopra